DIVINE REFLECTIONS
–OF–
INSPIRED ESSAYS AND POEMS
+++
The Spiritual Essence of the Holy Ghost's Presence

Henrietta Davison

Published And Distributed By
Professional Publishing House
1425 W. Manchester Ave. Ste B
Los Angeles, California 90047
323-750-3592
Email: professionalpublishinghouse@yahoo.com
www.Professionalpublishinghouse.com

Cover design: TWA Solutions.com
First printing November 2015
978-0-986-1557-4-1 (Paperback)
Library of Congress Control Number 201595726
10987654321

DIVINE REFLECTIONS
DEDICATED TO:

My daughter Mary Maxine Aimes and my son, Barry Dale Miller [both deceased] and to my Grandchildren; Jonnie Carolyn Frierson Gholar~Kimberly Roshaun Neal~Ylanda Cherie Wright~Clarence Dwaine Garland~Amanda Nicole Miller-Morgan~and John-Mark Miller-Davison\son-Grandson.
~Inclusive~
Great-Grandchildren: Anthony Jerone Gholar~Antionne Gholar~Jerry Mayle, Jr.~Areshanae Tierra King~Maccaia Iown Rose-Aminifu~Kiison Roujay McAlister and Ananda Tanae McAlister [twins]~Omari Dijon Garland~Lucretia Christina Garland-Corby …

My Great-Great~Grandchildren: Kaiilah Williams~Jair Tyner~Jerry Mayle, II~Aaleigha Corby~and Micah Corby.
~AND~
To all of my siblings: Marcella Washington, Vonceille Roberson, Mardell Loyd, Christine Johnson, Gail Henderson, William John Henderson, Jr., including my deceased siblings: Roxie Mae Douglas, Kwillard Henderson, Lady Joyce Quillopo, and a sister friend Claudia Royster and also an acknowledgement of all their children … family … a host of friends who encouraged, urged and pushed me on this path of writing … while trudging on my journey … AND STILL~I trudge!
I THANK YOU~~I LOVE YOU~~I THANK YOU!

MomsDear
Evangelist, Henrietta Davison~Poetess
August 10, 2015

"A SPECIAL THANKS"

I was chagrined, when I realized that I had not acknowledged a very significant occurrence in my first book, and had it not been for the Holy Spirit using this special person–and her willingness to be used; I am sure my first book would not have been written; thereby the door for my second book would not have been opened, either!

Subsequently, to my debut as a poetess, at the Central Baptist Church's prayer breakfast; this young lady came up after by recital, and some others, also; asking if I was published. However, my thoughts were racing, "Am I supposed to be? Oh, my Lord!" Finally I regained by composure, and said, "No, I'm not." But I remembered her persistence as she told me that the minute I write my book, she was in line to buy it. She had indeed planted a "seed" and it was powerful, in as much as; I couldn't forget, because it kept ringing in my ears–"Write a Book"–until it became a pressure and whether, I felt that my writing was worthy or not; I had to make the attempt, because she was waiting on my book!!

This happened on March 20, 1999 and I completed my first book [ever!]–in September 1999. Well, so many things happened while I tried to find her, and in my inquiry; no one knew who I was talking about. Later, I met this young lady at a civic function, and she asked me if I had 'written the Book'? I was so elated that I found the lady again, and took her name and telephone number, so, for sure, I would get the 'Book' to her,–right?...Wrong!! I lost the paper that I scribbled the information on! But finally!–finally!! last year, 2001–I met her again, at a social event and "thank the Lord"; I had a book with me!! She kept her word, even tipping me on the next book. I should have been tipping her!!! What do you think?

With lots of apologies and more than that...love for her quiet per-sistence. I want my reading audience to meet this beautiful person that God used...

Mrs. Eileen Washington!!
May God richly bless you and your family!

CONTENTS

Introduction 11

My Prayer [dedication] 19

Memorable 21

Dedication to My Family 23

I Can/I Am 25

God Pointed His Finger...35

The Man..50

We Are the Little People 51

Chile 2..52

The Millennium Women...58

Touch Upon 66

The Amazing Grace...68

Sarah 71

Stop the Violence 73

The Lying Beast 76

The Origin of The Phoenix 84

The Phoenix 86

Foreword Brother's Keeper 93

Am I My Brother's Keeper 95

Foreword Big Foot 99

Big Foot 101

Holy Spirit 111

The Holy Ghost...117

Memorial To a Special Niece 123

The Cover Story 125

MEDLEY I

Infancy to Infinity in the Shadow of His Hand
    Introduction 129
A Decree of Blessings...139
A Rose..141
Above the World 143
Crucified..144
Dear Pastor and Wife...146
God's Platinum Soldiers...148
Hear The Baby Crying..150
Foreword I Have Looked For You..153
I Have Looked For You Poem...155
In Remembrance of Mothers 156
No Lead ~ Hot Lead...158
No Words 159
Foreword O' My Gentle Breeze...161
My Gentle Breeze Poem 163
The Love of Life...164
The Stopping of the Clock 166
The Visitor..168
What Is Love 170

MEDLEY II

Signs Of The Times..181
A Blessed Birthday..188
The Blessed One...191
I Count My Blessings 193
The Blooming Flower...195
A Call To Order To Serve Pastor Bush 197

A Chosen Life 201

Death Has No Hold 203

Degree'd 205

Dedicated ~ Pastor Butler and First Lady 209

The Perfect Birthday Eternally 216

My Father Reminds Me..218

There Is No Greater Love 220

My Friend ~ My Second Skin 222

God's Stepladder In Place 225

Jess 230

The Beginning of Healing 231

A New Journey 233

The Live Doll 236

Sister-Sister Friend...239

A Suffering Servant 241

Slow Down Chariot 246

Waves Of Sorrow 248

Happy Father's Day...250

Funny~Funny 251

Distractions 261

Agers 271

The Battle Belongs To The Lord..280

Conclusion 282

Letters/Acknowledgements/Endorsements 284

About the Author..291

A Turn Of The Century Of Divine Reflections

☙ INTRODUCTION ❧

I thought that my first book would be a "back yonder-when" novel; but, God chose to have me do my first serious writing in epic poetry. He used my pastor to direct me into it. Pastor, Earline Neal, asked me to write a church creed, denoting grace and restoration. I had only one previous request to write an item, prior to her asking, which I had tried to refuse. My friend said, "I want you to write something for my album", "I can't write, Myles", I complained. After all, this man was a gold and platinum song writer and I felt that he could get a professional writer that could better compliment his album of songs. He retorted, "Well, I say that you are a writer, Miss 'D' and I want you to do the cover for my album." Needless to say, I was flabbergasted! Was he speaking of me!...a novice!, that only wrote for my own emotional outlet? After procrastinating for several months, I had a vision that he had come to pick up some writings that I was doing and I didn't have it ready. He paused and suddenly started walking out of a big gate or opening and I called to him and said that it was almost ready, but he said, "I can't wait Miss. 'D', I have to go!" and when I ran to overtake him; he was out of the opening or gate and was moving toward a vast space of nothingness. I awaken into a panic...which left me with a feeling that I must make an attempt to write something...and quick!

I prayed for the directions of the Holy Spirit. It came out as, "The Man", which is included in this book as a dedication to him, Myles Gregory. Subsequent, to presenting it to him, I discovered that he had cancer and succumbed on December 31, 1996. He was very pleased at the writing and presented it for reading to everyone that came into the hospital, I was told. His family included it as part of his obituary.

11

I, also, had a dream about Pastor Neal, asking me to do some kind of paper work that I saw myself doing; which is the reason that I could not say, "No, I don't feel that I am qualified," when she asked me to do the church tenet; because the Lord had already revealed the work to me. The Holy Spirit moved upon the writing of the "Amazing Grace" and opened the door, designating me as one of His conduits for other messages to flow through, as a poetess.

For years, I had written, sporadically, when I was emotionally moved to do so...and would just throw it away; later, someone told me I should keep them...some, I did...and will incorporate them as part of these current writings...along with poems that were inspired by special people and special events.

Somehow, these current poems were different...and I didn't know what to call them...because to me, they were more than just mere poems; my feelings and expressions had more depth. The Holy Spirit revealed to me, I was writing epic-poetry.

My son, John-Mark, decided he wanted to memorize "The Amazing Grace." God had already anointed the poem and consequently, he anointed his recital of it; causing him to be invited to churches and gatherings to orate. This promoted a chain reaction. Thereafter, I was asked to do writings on 'women', that I call "I Can/I Am" and "The Millennium Women", which were to be orated at the three million women walk. Both, have been incorporated in this book.

I have some of my mother characteristics, especially, when it comes to the 'age thang!' Therefore, when everyone was saying I was 'too old' to be rearing a child; I would come out with some of my mother's strong clichés, "Nothing gets old but clothes!" "Age ain't nothing but a number!" "You are as old as you feel!"...but my favorite one is my own expression, "God didn't think so, when He gave this child to me!"...and the peppy colloquialism goes on...but 'feel' was my key word...if I don't 'feel' it... then age is not problematic. But one day...

oh-h one day! This kid carried me through...like clothes going through an old wringer washing machine...so waterless, that the pieces could stand alone. This was the day when I groped my way to my bed, completely lethargic. As I lay there, I thought, "Lord, I think my friends may be right, I am too 'ole for this chile'! So, out of this weaken condition, came these two pieces, "Chile 1 and 2"...I am, only, including "Chile 2" in this book.

My stinger goes out when I hear about violence of the children. My thoughts are; we should have interpreted the handwriting on the wall before it started to consume us...and when my emotions reached the pinnacle of intensity...I said, "I got to write about this!" and while my feelings were being tugged ... I began to write, but, wait! it keeps rapping on me; actually, I dislike rapping with a passion, [or I did], but the Holy Spirit enlightened me to the fact, that the kids would listen to the words, if it was rapped...so the "Stop the Violence" rap song was birthed. It is being included in these writings. Now, I have more respect for the 'Rapsters'; if they are imparting positive messages, to our youngsters. I have overcome the preconceived notions of rapping as being ugly and have been blessed, subsequently, to consummate the epic poetry on...yes, you guessed it!...The same pet peeve; the violence of our children and it titled "The Lying Beast." It is the last piece that I have done, as of this date. It is completed and included as part of this collection of epic poetry.

Now, when someone ask if I am a poetess, I humbly, accept the title, unwaveringly; because God has blessed me with an anointed gift of poetry...I am humbled...and with that same perception; I could, unequivocal, answer a certain reporter's question, when he asked me, point blank, "What makes you think that you are a poetess?" And I answered, right to the point, "I don't think...I am! God has given me the gift and talent." Well, at that very moment, I came in to the full realization and acceptance of my gift, as being a poetess and writer... how 'good' or how 'bad' is determine by the eyes and ears of my audience.

The narrating of a subject matter, which is done in rhythmic story form, holds the attention and interest of the audience. I, particularly, enjoy orating dramatic pieces with a musical background!

My grandson, Waine, also hears the euphonious of poetry and has been blessed with the gift of writing; so I will include one of his pieces, called "The Visitor" by his request, in this book.

I walked right into my new writing career, when I moved here to Beckley, West Virginia. I am meeting people who God has put in my pathway to encourage and jostle me, into action. They are very special friends; Joyce Seabrook, a published writer; the authoress of "My Bout with Lupus, a Healing From the Son", always let me know that she is here for me, and sees that I am literarily and spiritually nourished by involvements.

My pastor, Earline Neal, seemingly, reveals messages in her sermons that say, "Just write down something to get started"..."Stop procrastinating"..."Your gifts will always make room for you and set you in high places before kings and queens", so, I curtsy to all of you, who read my book. Pastor Roosevelt Neal's, message rang out loud and clear, "Start where you are...use what you got...and do the best you can!" Well, after leaving church with these powerful words going around in my head...I would be gung-ho! "I've got to get started"...gotta put something down on paper! I would be so excited and overwhelmed about getting started on my writing; that I would just come home...eat and take a long nap!

Now, there are my friends, Clemmie and Williams Hinton, who are very encouraging; they have put up with me, practicing my poem reading on them; I think finally, she said, "Let me find someone else, who will listen to her", so she launched a prayer breakfast at her church...

invited some people to come and hear me...that way, she and Williams' ears got some rest! Whew!...

Later, I met Barbara Charles; who I call a 'mover and a shaker' because she is a lady that gets an idea about something and take action at the same time. She is, also, a writer and has strongly encouraged me; saying that I have some natural talents and compared me to a famous person, that shall remain nameless, because it's awesomely far-fetched... but, it indeed, teased my ego!

My friends, in California, have always been extremely supportive in all of my endeavors, whether they agree with them or not, they let me know, in no uncertain terms, that they are there for me. When the 'chips' are down...they are there...when things are looking 'up'...they are there...when I left them and moved out here...they are there...and here is spirit...

I hold them all close to me as being very dear. I will list some of them, as honorable mention, without going into the history of the friend-ships...that is, not until I write my next book. Starting from the oldest relationships are my dear friends: Leola Johnson, Ida Belle and Teely Rhyne, Sue Jamison, Claudia Morgan, Donna Bracy, Barbara Lousteau, Kathy Lousteau, Pamela Allen, Lynne Carter, Murlene Betty Streeter, Evangelist Cooper, Deaconess Mary C. Waters, Deacon Howard and Virginia Taylor, Deacon Allison and Bertha Owens, Phyllis Beasley, Joyce Westbrook and Milton Devore...all have made contributions of encouragement and prayer, in one way or another. Also, the endearment of others; who are a part of my church family in Altadena, California... Minister Wayne Bagby, Missionary Saundra Bridges, Deaconess Dwayla Williams, Lisa Austin and Pastor Henry Cos...my love encases the entire church family...and we keep them held up in prayer. John-Mark's Godfather, Dr. Nicholas Benson, who is in our prayers. We welcome and appreciate each one's encouragement and prayers.

Last...but, no ways...least...is my family, who stands by me and supports me in this gigantic step of moving here, to West Virginia. However, it was hard to get them to realize that God was pushing me out of their 'nest'! And he was sending me on another brand new path, of my journey. My children...[I lost my son, Barry, after my move, here...a shocking hurt indeed!] my daughter, Maxine, and my grandchildren, Carolyn, Kimberly, Waine, and Yolanda, keeps me uplifted with their love and concern. My mother, Charlotte, expired since I move here, which was also painful! My sisters, Roxie, Marcella, Lady Joyce, and my brother, Kwillard, and my cousin, Virginia, keeps in constant touch with me. None of them know what my next move will be, and of course, I can't tell them, because I don't know, either!!! But the journey is fun- even though, there are some bumps and rough spots in the road; I am learning how to rise above them, like when you ride a bucking horse and lift your body up from the saddle.

Any names of persons that have been missed, is not deliberate, and you are included in this list of well-wishers...just move your names to the top, because I love you all!

I thank God, continually, for each and every one of you, who is instrumental- in some way- of blessing me- as I walk on through.

I give a place of honor to Carl Burrows, an artist, who paints and teaches painting. I ask him if he would paint this beautiful picture of a tree, that you see on the front of this book...and he did. After he had completed it, I asked him, "How much do I owe you? He said, "You don't owe me nothing", I said, "Nothing!" He said "Nothing!" I looked at him and said, completely in unbelief, "But you can't do that!!" He said, "Girl, I can do anything, I want!" Finally, in amazement, I gasped, "I'm sorry! Sure you can! Thank you! Thank you!" as I walked out of his place, I was praising and thanking the Lord; not because of not having to pay for the paintings, [well, of course, that too!] but, primarily, I could see and feel, "God Pointing His Finger" as He guided me into writing this book! Hence, I have written the epic poetry with this title, which I have included in this book.

On a hunch a few years, ago; I decided to submit an item to the famous poet society. Perhaps, to find out whether others would find it interesting enough to read, or not...testing the waters, we may say. In a span of time, I received a letter stating my poem was selected and was invited to the Famous Poet Society's convention to receive the award. I read this and threw it aside, saying, "junk mail!" and forgot about it, until one day, I decided to do some cleaning, and ran across the letter. Finally, after toying with the idea, should I take it seriously, or throw it away..."Hey!" I thought, "You have nothing to lose, call!" The person whom I talked with, assured me that the letter was authentic and out of four hundred plus, only two hundred plus was accepted for the award... and my submission of "We Are The Little People" was one of those selected, to receive "The Diamond Homer Award". The poem was inspired by my son, John-Mark. I will include it in the collection of writings of this book.

"Touch Upon" was another emotional outburst that was vented on paper; when my loving pastor elder Edward Streeter, of Pasadena, California, went into an immediate coma. I didn't get a chance to ask him about his vacation, after they returned home. The two families always checked in, when the other returned from out of town. I told my husband, we will check tomorrow. On that date he was comatose. It took a long time for me to bring closure to his death...I didn't get a chance to say??????? I try not to wait on doing things, "ma~nana", [pronounced as mon-yana-meaning...tomorrow] since then. The poem was written on his obituary and I have enclosed it as a part of these writings.

Prior to compiling the epic poetry for this book...I felt the title should be "Divine Reflections"...but I had a dream that said, name it "Turn of the Century", which I added "Divine Reflections"...so my book title is "Turn of the Century of Divine Reflections."

I hope and pray that these writings of epic poetry will be enjoyed because they are written in the Spirit of the Lord and from the innermost being of my heart!

MY PRAYER

OH FATHER...I thank you again and again for **enlarging** my borders...
You have kept your hand upon me–since the beginning of my time
Here on earth
My whole life you did see–also, my family...
You have nurtured and brought us...this far.
You have given me time to enjoy my grandchildren–
Yea!...even my great-grands.
Thank you Father–God for mental adeptness–physical sturdiness–emotional soundness–and spiritual progression.
And I continually give you praise, honor and glory in Jesus, your son and my [Our] Savior's name–Who lives **within** me with his **power, strength, hope, light, love and mercy**...
Being my intercessor with you, my Father. He directs my path through the divine power of the Holy Ghost–who continues to work in my life to make–positive and spiritual change.
Oh **Holy Spirit,** I thank you, incessantly, for being my **companion, keeper**–my **comforter** and **teacher**–my **counselor** and **interpreter**–who directs and guides me–always present through all known and unseen–troubles.
You have opened doors–that I never thought possible to walk–therein...
Doors that I had read about...fantasies of extensive travels–you opened the door–

And said, 'Go'! You have blessed me with homes–businesses and some luxury cars.

You have blessed me with good jobs...and floors of clothes.

Any you are indeed blessing my writings!!

As you are blessing me with good spiritual–physical–mental and emotional health.

But, Father–none of these compare with the gift of the **Baptism of the Holy Ghost** and His presence, continually! I can never do without Him!!...A precious gift manifested–here in Beckley, West Virginia...**and I thank yo**u!

And Jesus, I thank you for the stripes that you took for me [and all of us] that my body is **constantly healing**...and I magnify and glorify your name, while you pray to the Father-God...for us...in your–interceding.

Oh Holy Ghost...I thank you...without your help–my writings would be lacking spiritual depth and embodiment. My understanding of the scriptures would not be coming alive–without you revealing them to me–while we are writing poetry.

And when I am weary–I can **talk to you** and **rest in you–upon you–through you**- you are **always welcome here!!!**

Jesus, I thank you for the **outpouring of your love**–into the center **of my being**...keeping me close to you from my very beginnings–as you mold.

I give you **reverence and praise...with everything that you have given me to praise and reverence you with!!!**

And–Oh! **Father-Son-and Holy Ghost!!!**...On you–I will, forever **trust...rest...and be depending!!**

I praise...honor and glorify Your Holy Names!!

A MEMORABLE TO MY
MOTHER-GRANDMOTHER AND SON

I thank you Mo'dear for teaching me the importance of knowing the Lord as my personal savior as you expounded upon the foundational teachings of my grandmother. Lenora Lampkins.

I thank you, Mrs. Scott, for teaching us to be independent, aggressive in business and being a pillar in helping to care for my children, when the chips were down. Also, you taught us that you never get too old...nor is it ever too late, to pursue your dreams...hence, here is my first book...small but nevertheless...a book! It shall be one among many! [I hear you being thrilled with this statement!].

I thank you, mama, and I thank God for making you my grandmother. You have had the greatest influence on my life as you were the model of richness in the midst of poverty...the excellence...in excelling in your endeavors...you espoused the value of education...you taught that the goodness inside of your heart...was important...not the outside appearance...to share with the less fortunate, even if it is meager...to love, not envy...nor 'throw stone for stone'. But, mama, I thank you most of all...for introducing us to God...and teaching us that He is a person that we can relate to...communicate with about our problems, our joys and sadness...and in all things, we can rely on Him.

Barry, I thank God for you, son, as being the integral part of my being. Your purpose of life was short, but potent. I thank, God, for blessing you with a son; thereby, my grandson and now, son; who is a strong catalyst of my life. God has blessed him with a special love for people...that's overwhelming...and a dynamic charismatic personality. In so many ways I see you in him. I thank you, son, for him. Trying? Yes! But the returns are more than money can buy...and that's God's love that shines within him.

This book memorializes each one of you.

Henrietta Davison–September 1999

DEDICATION TO
MY FAMILY–FRIENDS AND OTHERS

My Prayer

The Lord has blessed me with a loving family,
Caring friends and others;
He continues to bless...and connect me...
As I travel further;
With beautiful people...who sees...the I am/I can
'Being', who is looking for the key...
To open the doors of desti-ny.

I travel on this road to my –Damascus
Thanking God...and savoring...
Every word...smile and deed...
As I gather them all...in my grateful basket.
Each one is special...and a beloved favorite...
Which assists me in reaching...my destination...
That will fulfill my ultimate...creation!
I shall count these...as my blessings increase...
Before I leap!
Into my casket...
To sleep...

And I cry out...in my prayer

To my father...who I know is there...
O'Lord untwine this inner soul...
From the outer man...so that I may see...
The divine plan and infinite role...of my
Life's journey to the pre-destine goal...
My life's uncertainties are mere reflections of
My confusions...my consciousness tortures and
Twists my mind...with conclusions.
And with every turn on life's pathway...there are
Ups...downs and delusions.

O'Lord!, I am not importuning thee...for a lighter
Burden...nor do I qualify to peek thru the future
Curtain...and see...what should happen to
"O'pore me!"...

All I ask, O'Lord...is for enough
Strength...faith...courage and endurance...
To take each step of the way...with confidence...
Spiritual fortitude...and assurance!

Henrietta Davison–September 1999

I CAN/I AM

I can be...I am one...who walks alone...
dispersed in the universe
The sun I can see...shinning into the night...
as I run toward the light
While on this journey...I saunter
Thru the jungle...I wander
I am a wayfarer...and my soul...
is yearning...
To be somewhere...out yonder.

I can be...because I am...
A wo-man...that's blessed...
not damned!
Of course, I grope and cope...with my concerns...
Sure...I think...,sometimes, my purposes...
are my curses...
As my heart burns...when they surface...
thru my sufferings.

But!...I am- an amazing wonder!!...that causes the
universe to echo like thunder...
And the world to roll and rumble...while I nurture all
creations...as a natural nourisher...

I move boldly with courage...as I maneuver thru
contentions and confront dissensions...
And I eagerly search...upon this earth...
my spiritual identity...
While, slowly, slipping...into...
blissful infinity.

I am Eve...who was deceived and got reprieved...
Yes...I ate the apple on the tree...I even coaxed Adam
to eat with me...
But, Adam with a pious deception...
Mustered all the dignity...that he had left...
to defend his disobedient-self!
He exclaimed loudly, "The woman you gave me...
Call me a coward...so, I ate the apple...but...
I didn't eat the seed!"
However, God saw him do the wicked deed...as he
Consensually...broke the universal law.

I am a woman...who turned the world...
upside down...
While I twirled and whirled it...
all around.
I put man in a rebellious state...which was grounds for
eviction...from our paradise estate.
Yea...the same...who caused Satan...to crawl on...
his belly...
And eat the dirt like it's jelly...
Eternally slinking and slithering...
Thru all things that's smelly.
He did the wrong thing...when he went a-snake-n with me;
I-am Eve!! T h e   u n r u l y   s e e d!!!

Man did fall and all of that...but, God went to his creative vat...
And kneeling down on his designing mat...
Stirred up a composite...of fire and brimstone...
That resembled a...crimson dome...
The melting pot was exceedingly hot...
When he slung it into a much hotter spot.
As it blasted into outer space...it divided into many tiny cells...
Separating time...and place, as it fell...
Forming the eternal...pit of hell.

Because of this loss...of sweet bliss...
I am a woman...who is faced with this;
Subject and submerged...
I cannot act alone,
My identity and femininity...
Thru my mate...I belong;
And while I am commanded to replenish the earth...
I am disciplined thru painful...childbirth...

Howbeit...I can not be in defeat...because of Eve's deceit...
Jesus says...'in him.... I am complete'
He conveys that...I am Sara...a mother of nations...
Not limited to special races...
In him is the creation...that's also...in me...
Procreating human form...of all kinds;
Kings, queens and princes...with great minds...
Logicians and politicians that...challenges and convinces
Doctors, prophets, preachers...lawyers and teachers...
Presidents, judges and servants...
The blind, weak, sick and ...afflicted...
Even murderers, thieves and derelicts...
And con-men...who are full of tricks
These are throngs of only a few...that belongs to me, too.

I am the door that they came thru!...a circle of life...
none can eschew!
I am a woman...who is shrewd and astute...
I created the 'I can institute'
I am a minister and servant to all...
There is no dispute that I am...called...
I exude intense propensity of absolution...
These attributes...are some of my...contributions.

I am Deborah the judge...who rode with Barak...
in his chariot...

He was God's chosen chattel that was called to do his battle.
I shielded his spineless backbone...making sure that...
nothing would go wrong.
Cause God was preparing for a special moment...
To use the hands. of a gentle woman...
To nail the head...of the enemy down...
level unto the ground.

I am Jael the woman used...to drive a heavy tent nail...
thru Captain Sisiera's head...
God endowed me. a frail female...
with his power...
To show he is the awesome-tower!

I am Jezebel, the prophet killing wench...
I had a thirst for death...that couldn't be quench.
It was my scheme. To have Naboth stoned...
To take his vineyard and home
Prophets lives were wrenched...
While I filled the country side...with their stench!
As I rule with...Aplomb!

For these dastardly deeds...I had to pay...
So, from my throne...I was snatched...one day!
And out of my window...I was thrown.

Now, no one cared...nor dared to hinder...
My flesh from becoming...mulch and cinders.
This atrocity, was true...to prophesy;
Brought to memory...when the thud...
of my dumped body was heard...
And the sounds of the dogs...
slurping my blood.

They gnawed and gnashed...my broken bones...
But my skull, hands and feet...
Were left...as I moaned
For another mealtime...these choice morsels were kept
Cause they couldn't hold...any more to eat...

I am Ruth...a sojourner from Moab...
Who made my home with Naomi...
where the conditions were drab...until...
I met and married her cousin...Boaz
My life with him was...the reason...
For my destiny to be...
the ancestress...of Jesus.

I am Rehab the harlot of Jericho...
Who hid Joshua's spies...behind my door...
I am an ancestress...
of the Messiah.

I am Dorcas...a disciple of Joppa...
full of good works...and almsdeed...

Made coats and garments for those...in need...
And raised from the dead...by Peter, the Apostle...
When he kneeled and prayed...
by the side of my bed.

I am Anna, the Prophetess...who prophesied over his life...
As I confirmed and witnessed...that Jesus was...
the Christ.

I am Vashti...the Queen...who paved the way...
for Esther...
The King set me aside...when I refused to abide...
In his presence...as he had requested.
immediately...he put me in sequester.

I am Queen Esther, who won the love of the king...
He was eager to please...since Vashti wasn't
there...to appease.
However, I have no peace.
At this very moment...plans are being made...
to kill my people...and to enslave.

For you see, Haman the wicked one...
Being full of corruption...
Has ordered our destruction.
It was of the utmost importance...to expose what...
he had done...
I sought for an audience...a banquet was prepared...
Only Haman and the king...were invited
to be there...
In the palace...on the left wing.
On food and wine...Haman splurged...
Until, his evil plot was...divulged.

The king was very upset...and went outside to fret...
But only ordered him dead...when he caught him on
my bed!
Since, this act was so callous...he was sent to die...
on his own gallows...
Fifty cubits high...that he had made...
for Mordecai.

His neck hung loose in the noose...as his body swung...
above the scaffold.
He gasped for air...his eyes bulged in a...stare...
He tried to swallow...even holler...
When his head flung...the body plunged...
And the legs jerked...above the shallow cavity...
That waited to engulf...the flesh...of depravity...
There in the evening...shadows.

I am Mary, blessed above all women...
Conceive the Christ child...
by the holy spirit.
He was the "word" carried in my womb...
'Til birth...so all men could...hear it.
The heavens were prepared as my...delivery room...
While, the angels rejoiced and...began to croon.
Their singing was heard upon the earth...
and from high above...
Causing the wise men to find...the child...
of love...

I nourished him from my paps...as I held him...
in my lap...
Strong and sturdy...into adulthood...he grew.
Then, I watched him sup from the bitter cup...

And the sufferings...he went thru...
As his footsteps were being ordered...
to the cross...to save the loss.

I watched him die...and saw the darkened...sky...
And while, the earth was quaking...and his cross shaking...
All of the fears of the passing years...
Moved across my face...as drowning tears!!

I witnessed the third day...when he arose...
from the grave...
No longer, could he be held there...
in the burial cave.
He gave his life...and now we are reprieved...
From death and hell...he took the...keys.
His mission of grace was well achieved...
And our father was exceedingly...pleased!

I am Mary Magdalene...with seven devils...
That are dwelling in me...on different levels.
Jesus called...and cast each one...out!
Now, I am free!...I am happy!
It makes me sing and...shout!

I was the first one to see him...after he had arisen...
The message delivered by me...to them...
was Jesus' decision...
"Go tell my brethren...I ascend to my father and
Your father...my God and your God"...
Referring to our spiritual father...in heaven.

I ran and danced with the message...

It was vital and refreshing...
"Jesus is with us!"...I, loudly, cried
He, yet, lives!! He is alive!

I am now...a black slave...mus' lurn hy-tuh...
tawk an' b'haabe!!
I kin ply bet'n eny man! Plaint an' pik kotun...
'tell I ba'ly kin stan'...
I kin tak' my blo's an' likkins...whe' eb'r...
dey lan'!
Burth mi ba-bees...n' mi o'n hans...
Wa'ch dem takin'...whi' day don' un'erstan'...
Tuh be beet'n 'n pok'd...
wid hot I'on bran's...

My har's a'pump'n...bleed'n...my guts twiss'n...
an'tunn'n...!
My hed's spinn'n ise's budgin'...rollin'...and jump'n...!
Kant sa' nuddin'...kant do nuddin'...
but mi so'I screems...!!!
Pant'in...wid hush moanin's!
Now...I ask...as many loud voices...
and in many tongues...
Infusing with the same questions...of
Sojourner truth's...Confusion...
"But...ain't I a woman!!!!"

I can be!!...because I am!!...the main artery of the
Potter...
That God uses...as a conduit...for human life to flow...
thru it!
He graced me with sensitivity and enveloped me

with love and gentility.
I am enlarged with a heart of compassion...
that's caring, sharing...even daring.
While my soul is preparing...to transform into...light...
I am being lifted to new heights...with complete fullness...
and spiritual insight.
I perceive my eternal destiny...while moving into infinity...

As I gravitate towards the center...of my God's heart...
where the pumping of his love first...
Started...because he is the ...highest tower...
of omnipotent power!!!

GOD POINTED HIS FINGER

The finger of God pointed to the stars...
as he was trying to choose
"No...maybe the sun or the moon...
Can't make up my mind...
which one to use..."
"No...none of these heavenly bodies will do...
Not even the angels, who would be
absolutely...enthused"

Then his finger pointed towards the earth...
Out into the vastness...
of the universe...
I know--let's make man...in our own image and likeness!"
And the creature was created in the godhead's...
exactness.

Then, he ran his hand across the sand...
Picked it up and...momentarily...
let it stand...
Subsequently---sifting it slow-ly...
to the ground.
It was soft and smooth-th...falling into little pools...
as he knelt down...
Patting and shaping...making it round.

"Ah-h yes!! Then he began to knead and puddle the dirt...
thumping in a big lump of love...as he stirred.
Carefully, he outlined the physique...until the task was...
complete.
He called softly...man!...oh man!!
Suddenly! The flesh quickened...within his hand...
coming alive...upon his command.

He took his finger and pointed again..."Get up man!...
I want you to stand!"
Man got up under the power of God's hand...
He said, "Now walk!" He began to walk...
with a rock...like a robot.
God's finger pointed again...and he said, 'Now man talk!"...
he did...under the power...of God's voice.

Then God thought, "What's wrong with man...
On his own...he doesn't...understand?"
He put his finger under his chin...and begin to think...
"Hum-m-m" then he figured out...
the missing link...
An breaking out into a big grin!..."Oh-h-h! Now I know...
He's not quite done...he needs some fire!...
So that he can know...my desire!"
And God breathe...into his nose...
and man became a living soul!
Male an d female...he made them...
Later separating...her from him.

Then one day...God pointed his finger...
calling out to them...to come to him...
As they lazed and played...in joyful frolic
In the coolness of the day...there under the shade...

of the tree of knowledge.
Instantly!...their flagrant folly...was revealed and their
Nakedness could not...be concealed.
So, they hid in the quietness...of the gentle breeze...
Where the act of disobedience...was first conceived.

God got busy...he was furious...
Made them coats of rough hide...
And untanned skin...
His children had committed their first
disgraceful sin...
God can't lie...they had to die.

He didn't want them to feel comfortable ---
nor look...richy...
Because the spirit...that was exhibited...
Had to be restrained and...restricted.

As they were covered...he pointed his finger
toward the gate...
'O' man of dust...let's get one thing straight!
Obedience- is a must...anything less...
will not be tolerated!
Albeit...this is your chosen fate...
So, fend and depend on each other...I~I~I!!!--
will not support you, further!"
And then with a shout...he kicked them out!!!...'
Far from him...he routed them...thru the exit...
of the Garden of Eden.
They carried knapsacks...on their backs...each filled with
curses...(quoting a small portion and paraphrased, thusly)...
"As you dwell upon earth, man,...you will eat by the sweat...
from the brows.

Woman, your childbirth will be...with sorrows and wailing...
howls"
This was the fate of them...and their future kin.
He pointed his finger at Abraham...
to sacrifice his son, Isaac.
Well, Abraham went up to obey...
because he was very pious.
He built the alter...though, he faltered...
Counting each twig of wood...trembling, as he stood...
He built the fire...his son was tied...
All preparation was made...for him to die.

Abraham, the father...had a heavy heart...
Because God's order...could not be bartered...
After, he had run out of excuses...he pulled out
his knife and got ready...to use it...
Holding blindly to his faith...as his heart pounded and raced.
His hands shot up in mid air...holding the knife...high...
Ready to bring it down...to take his son's life...
Eyes closed...he had a death pose...
Suddenly!...he heard a rustling noise...
and the angel saying, "Abraham!
Do not slay him...look in the bushes...under a limb...
there—you will find the sacrificial...Ram!"

The finger of God pointed to Ship'rah and Puah...
The Hebrew midwives...of the Israelites...
"Just say no...to the commands of old pharaoh...
to do his dirty and bloody chore...
The sons...you must not slaughter...and do continue...
to save the daughters.
"Well, they feared God...more than pharaoh...
so they lied, saying, "The Israelite woman are more lively...

And don't wait for delivery by...midwifery."
So, God dealt well with them...for obeying him...
and the baby sons of Israel...survived...
and rapidly...multiplied.
Then pharaoh...took matters into...his own hand...
sending orders...all around...
That sons in the land...must be drowned.

Jochebed decided to hide her child...and was led...
To the river brink...of the Nile.
There she made an ark of bulrushes...
in the shape of a little...crib bed...
Sealed with slime and pitch...pile high and...thick...
So, that it wouldn't shrink...nor sink...
And there would be no crushes...while the river rushes.

God pointed his finger...so that pharaoh's daughter could see...
The little ark as it...bobbed and weaved.
And sent her maidens to fetch it...where the water receded...
She saw a comely Hebrew child...and knew that
a mother had sacrificed...
And when he cried...she was moved to...compassion...
As he held unto her hand...with tenacity.

She called him "Moses"...saying, "Because I drew
him from the water."
Unaware that he had been chosen...by the heavenly father.
Then, the baby began to chortle...and in those days...
did they have bottles?
Howbeit...his sister...pharaoh's daughter's maiden...
was hastened...to search...for him, a wet nurse.
Naturally, she brought their own mother...
With her identify disguised...she was hired...

And while the nation was shuddering with...
children's murders.
She was being blessed as her child's nurturer...
Paid a wage...until he grew up to be...
of...weaning age.

God pointed his finger...had Moses driven out...from his
comfortable home...
And put him in a combat zone...to prepare him for the
purpose...and the reason that...
he was born.
God had a plan...that was brilliantly strategic...
To deliver his people...from the bondage of Egypt.

As Moses was use to lead the Israelites...
Pharaoh put up a vigorous fight...
When God pointed his finger...there was no equal
match...for his might.
After many cataclysmic disasters...
Pharaoh succumbed...to defeat...
And did a temporary...retreat.
The Israelites...he gladly release...to their God
Who had...divine authority.

Again...God pointed his finger...to open and close the Red
Sea...
To help his people cross...by drowning their ene-my.
The white waves rolled and tossed...as they engulfed and
swallowed...everything that was not hallowed...
Horses...chariots and armored men...caught up
As if in a whirlwind...until everyone was...fatally...
loss...
Making mammoth meals for the hungry...caws.

God pointed his finger...to write the ten commandments...
for his people had become...quite outlandish...
He wrote on two tables of stone...
to define the difference...between...right and wrong.
Well–Moses couldn't scoot down the mountain...
fast enough...
To stop them from worshipping a golden calf...
He could hear their laugh...
While doing a lot of crazy...stuff.
When Moses saw this...he went into a...hissing fit...
He smashed the recorded tables...into tiny bits.
Then he had to sit...to get himself calm...
Because he felt like doing them bodily...harm.
As he collected his...composure...
he, suddenly, had a disclosure...
And sprinted back up the mountain...
to give God an accounting...and
With incoherent babbles...he ask him to rewrite...
TWO MORE TABLETS.
Well–God recognized...that Moses was not...
infallible
And...that the children of Israel...were stiff neck...
as heck...
With heads as hard...as rocks and...cinder blocks...
Therefore, he complied...had Moses to cut out two
tables of stones...
Like the first ones...that he had thrown...
And God said, "Make an ark to put them in"...
and the rewriting...did begin.

God pointed his finger...and said..."Samuel–stop mourning
for Saul...for whom I rejected.
  Go to...the Bethel-mite...whose name is...Jesse...

He will be a king with my...insight.
Well, Samuel had a time...picking out the right one...
as each of the seven...passed in a line.
He said, "None of these are chosen from heaven."
Then he sent for the youngest...of the eight...
The family's sheep keeper...who was standing...at the gate.

When God pointed at David...
Samuel obeyed...poured upon his head...
the anointed oil...
David, then was filled...with the spirit of the Lord...
And the moment was sacred...while his destiny was assured...
of being royally...majestic!

God pointed his finger...to the forefront of the...
Israelite's battleground...
Where David heard a big booming...
sound...
From Goliath of Gath...a boisterous echo...
that floated down...the mountain path.
His challenge caused the Israelites...
To quake in fear and...tremble...
But when David heard...his wrath...
was kindled.
The giant was huge...a span and six cubits high,
Who was unaware...that he was getting ready...
to die.
With his coat of mail...and heavy
battle gear...
He strutted like a rooster...
as he scoffed and jeered!

God pointed his finger...to five smooth stones...
for David to choose...
Only one...he needed to use...
He slang it hard...in the name of God...
As it whizzed and sank...into the giant's...forehead.
Dramatically, he fell flat on his face...
bone stiff...and quite dead!!...
David was bold...he took the giant's sword...
and used it to hack off...his burly head.

After running from Saul, a number of years
Thru blood, sweat, wilderness...and tears ---
God pointed his finger...again...for David to take
his throne...as king...
And all over Israel and Judah...
his name ranged...with great reverence and fame.
David indeed had human flaws...but he was next...
to God's own...heart...
So, he established his throne forever...
Beyond his expectations...and endeavors.

God pointed his finger...at three Hebrew men...
Who were sent to die...in a furnace of...fire...
King Nebuchadnezzar's orders were ...to bake them...
Because they refused to obey him...
in honoring his god...the golden...image.
They said, "Our God, we will not...forsake!"
As they defied...in verbal scrimmage...
Well. The king's anger flared and...
did escalate.
He, then, commanded his mighty men
to throw them...in...

The burning furnace...made seven times...
hotter...
That couldn't be quenched...
By a river of water!

The militia dragged...the clothed
Shadrach--Meshach--and Abednego...
close...to the burning lip...ready to ...throw...in their...
struggling hips...
Too quickly...they let go and slipped!...
Into the flaming fire...at it leapt...higher...
Over the rim...to swallowed them!!
Of course, they were the ones baked...like a charred...steak!!

The Nebuchadnezzar took a look...and was amazed and rose
up...as if in a daze...
He saw them unarmed...not three...but four!
"But didn't we throw three men, (he asked) thru the burning
door?"

As he peered, he said, "The form of the forth is like the Son of
God!"
Well. He called out the heads of state...
They stared hard...ad gaped!
Then thoroughly checked...the Hebrew men...
Nothing was burned, nor a hair singed...
Not even the smell of fire was on...one thing!

Subsequently, 'ole nebby' made a decree that...
Every people, nation, language...
And creed...
Which spoke against the God of...
Shadrack, Mesach and Abednogo...

Would be cut into a...small portion...
and their houses made into dunghills' (Like today's landfills)
"There's not a God", he said, "to deliver...
after this sort!"...
And...then he shivered...at the very thought.
God had taught him a lesson...and got
His finger (oops!) point across...

God pointed his finger...and wrote on the plaster of King Bel-
shaz-zar's...Wall...but, the strange writings...he could not read
therefore, the message, he did not perceive...
Nor the astrologers...soothsayers and wisemen...
That he had called...
even though they were problem solvers.
The king was extremely worried...And troubled...
Because he hadn't been able...to find an...interpreter.

Well, the queen heard...ad came to comfort...her hus-band
She reminded him of the man...in his kingdom...that
He'd...renamed Bel-te' shaz-zar...
Who knew all about the heavens...
And the stars...
This man, also had the spirit of...
Holy Gods...
A goodly understanding and an interpreter...
Of dreams.
So, the king called him...
"Daniel", he said, "tell me...what these strange writings say...
and what it means."
Well, Daniel, deciphered the writings...
on the wall...
And the bottom line...was this...
That the king's kingdom was divided...

And would, certainly, fall...
And that very night...it crumbled...under the enemies' might!

God pointed his finger...at Daniel in the lion's den...cast there
by jealous men...
The angel locked the jaws...of the lions...and no manner of
hurt...was founded.
King Darius was exceedingly glad...
As the trumpets...resounded...
Demanding that Daniel be brought to him...and ordered his
accusers to be thrown in...over the rim of the den...
Along with their wives and...children...
By this time...the lions were...starving...
And were not frightened...by hysterical...sobbing.

God pointed his finger...and Jesus came on earth...
Thru the virgin Mary...as a holy birth.
His only begotten son...he sent into this...world...
So that our souls could be saved...
Through his grace and love.

God pointed his finger...intertwining it with his son's...
Instead of two...they became one...then Jesus pointed his
finger...in his father's name...

Since then---the world was never...
The same!

Jesus pointed his finger...and raised the dead...
He commanded Lazarus..."to come forth!"
Saying to Mary 'Unwrap his head...loose him and let him...
go!"

While he taught...a multitude of people...were fed...
He would bless and increase the loaves...of bread.
The 'Word' spreaded his light into the world...
As he walked and talked...healing the sick...
And touching souls...in such terrible...torment...
And the feeble pressed in...just to touch the hem of his
garment.

So, the scribes and Pharisees...got busy
Gathering evidence...against Jesus...
They used a woman of adultery...
For this insidious...reason...
And the law of Moses...was the tool...used...to accuse...
'Catching her in the very act'...meant that they had to
participate...as–'just a matter of fact' to...incriminate...
Why-y-y...they could kill two birds with...one stone...
'Enjoy it' and 'destroy it'...
Who would dare prove that they...also had done wrong?

Now, after their sport and spoil...they could present living
proof...
 Not realizing that they had goofed.
As Jesus was prodded for flaws...regarding...
Moses' laws...
He stooped down...without uttering...a sound...
Pointing his finger...he wrote on...the ground.
They persisted for an...answer...
And he rose and said, "He without sin among you...
Let him case the first stone...at her."
And stooped again...and with his fin-ger...
wrote on the ground...
They murmured with their heads...hung down;

while their conscience convicted...and condemned...them.
The varmints realized that the chicanery had failed...
and slithered away...hurriedly...
like whirl-winds were on their...tails!

Finally, Jesus lifted himself and said, "Woman, where are your
accusers? Hath no man condemned?"
Looking around for her abusers...and users...
She said, "No man, my Lord"!, of course not!
Realizing, that they had lost the gamble;
they, immediately, fled away on their camels...Jesus said,
"Neither do I...go and sin no more!"

God and son...point their fingers as one...
To bring the suppressed...
Thru the bloody slime...of inhuma-nistic crimes...
The oppressors stomping the oppressed...
Living in the likeness of...the flesh...
Refusing to admit and to realize...(even though)...it is
biblically chronicled...and recognized...
That we are divinely...intertwined...
and share common bloodlines.

Even so, the Cain and Abel mentality...still exists...
Brother killing brother...
Is not a new twist.
One ties the rope around the other's neck...
Lifting him up...from the...ground...
The other...that ropes his brother's neck...
Himself...is being plummeted low–and further–down.

God and his son...pointed their finger...one day...
And pushed me out of my comfort zone...
And sent me far away...
From my home...
Led me to Beckley, West Virginia...
And said, "This is where your journey will continue!!"
God and Son...points his finger...at you...you...and me, too!
Giving us daily lessons...to achieve the goals...
For the destiny of our souls.
And when we're still...we can hear him...converse...
As we step out into the spiritual...universe.
He directs us towards the true path...
That is filled with light and love...
While he guides us from within...
and high above!!

THE MAN

A man walking through...exploring his environs...full of queries and filled with boundless energies...gregarious with an **assertive persona**, yet, **kind and compassionate.**

He searches for **new frontiers...seeks new horizons** and **delights** in **contemporary discoveries**...being **analytical** in his quest for **knowledge**...as he **fraternizes** and **mingle with all**; whatever their status is on the social "totem pole." He carries himself with the **epitome of pride and dignity**, as he honors his **Words of promises.** His **beliefs** and **requests...captivates** and **convinces**...as he speaks with **quite authority.**

He appears to be an open book...but **his depth** cannot **be measured**... or weighed. Who is he...that can effortlessly, guard his identify, feelings and emotions...from all attempts to delve into his soul??

He commands respect as he **appeals** to the **altruistic nature** of others. A **man...seeking** and **making** his own **destiny**, while touching on the lives of his society...**marching** to his own drum beat...exuding confidence...staking **no claim** that he is a man...**he just is!**

He **stands** tall **and** strong against life's **adversities**...while walking through the valley of the shadow of death; he **handles** his oppositions... difficulties...responsibilities with **courage** and **determination!**

The man...who ask not...nor encourage **"sympathy sitcoms"**, but **embraces** the **odds...affirms** and **emphasizes** the **positive** and speaks the words of **life...living** and love...he is a man!!!

WE ARE THE LITTLE PEOPLE

We are the little people,
The fruits of the world;
Even though...we seem feeble...
Our bodies are constantly...in a twirl...

We are the future hope...
so you must be able to cope...
Protect...and guide...don't ever leave...
our side...
Put us on a Christian team;
'Cause all of these are needed...
to give us self-esteem.

Come...take us by our...little hands...
Show us the way...thru troubled lands...
Even though...we are small in stature...
Our minds can fully capture...
How you view us...when we are good...
or when we are bad...
Or making you happy...or...sometimes sad.

So...let us all be up ad doing...
Our father's business...
we are pursuing...
Whether...we are...a child...or an adult...
It is all about...the end result!!!

CHILE 2

They told me...they tol'l-d me!
"You too ole!!!...
Fer a chile!"
Stumblin' aroun'...yu now yuk ant see...to good...
de youngi's hidin'...
Look...in de woods...behin' the tree!
He's a movin' fas'...eber wheah! Ober heah!...ober dere'!...
Honey--whatcha' need...I'm jest gonna tel' ya whatcha...
Need-d...!
Is a li'l quie-et spot...wid ar bris' cuppa–whiski' tee...
An' ar ole rockin' chair...
Jes'ter rockin'...rockin'...an snoosin'...
An...lettin' God yuse yu!"...

And I said...I said with a flair...
"The Lord giveth and the Lord taketh...
and this chile wasn't given to me...as a spare...
It was because of how much...he cared
Besides...while blending the old with the new...each one can
help...the other one through.
Then...saying, with emphasis; "I trust in the Lord
Who strengthens!
He has made the choice...and with this chile...
I do rejoice!"

Since, I was 'On a roll'...I went into ...
melodramatics...assuring all...including myself...
That with this precious gift...
I am ecstatic!
Although, I have serious conversation with the Lord...regarding
his promise of...daily restoration.
I say, "This chile that you...gave me.
Keeps me down on...one good knee...
If you'll just help me...with this...
Little Blessing.
Calm down some of the hyperness...
Then, I can have a little more time of...
Rest and peaceful quiet-ness
And Lord...Lord! Hear my urgency...
Because I need healthy years for a...
Long-g-g while!...
So, that I can better deal with...this unruly chile!"

All the noises...the screeching sounds...
Squalling and bawling...kicking and running around...
Thumping--bumping and bouncing balls...there's no silence...
And very few...pauses...
Hurry now!! You have to cook...clean
and wash their drawers!
I heard them!...Un-hunh! I heard them!...
Job's compatriots...incarnated...
One said, "What's wrong with her?"...
And the other one..."Chile!!!
she's vi'-ratin'...a'ced-derat'n...an' shakin' like she needs to be
datin'"...
And then...the prognosticator...of the three..."Well!–mey-bee...
It's pawlsy or dat..."Pawkson d-sees"...!

Oh no!...they don't understand!
I don't have time to be sick...nor can I do as I please...
Can't they see God and this chile running...with my hand.
No longer...can I slow-w-ly get out of bed...
There is a certain scream and shriek...
A lightning bolt across...my head
that jolts me out of a deep sleep...
Don't have time to think...nor kick out...
The night's kinks...

It's out of the question...whether I can make it or not...
The chile needs a drink...have to hurry and warm the
bottle in the pot!

I never thought that...I could appreciate modern mamas...
Had often ridicule them for using pampers...and making their
babies wear bottom-less "Jamers"...
And the fact they couldn't stan-n-nd...to put their hands...
In the washing of the "icky" little dirty diteys...

"Humph!!" I said...I did say!! That's a bit
"High and mitey!...
In my day...there was no choice...in deciding...
You held your breath...put your hands in the mess...
And centuries of mothering...stood the test.

Of course, I could not see...what was in store...for me...
The coming trauma...of being a renewed 'Mama'...
Which was like staggering...fifty years...
Backward...
Or being on a roller coaster...jolting...
Lurching and jarring.

You begin to long for periods...to rest and lounge...
From the undue stress and excess pounds.
Well, some corners I had-d to cut...
Had to get out of the 'mama' Clutch.
The modern mom's tendency...to be trendy...
Had some merit...and suddenly...I was comprehending...
Because, at first; I thought...they were plain lazy!
But...listen...it's my third time around...
Of child raising...
And, now, I have joined this generation
Of' short stops'...
Just snatch it off...and sling it in the trash!...
Or...some other easy drop!...

I have more reason than they do...
Cause I thought that I was through...
Hey! They're on to a good thing!!...I ain't crazy!!

No more trottin, tipping and toeing...
And looking cute...with pearly white teeth...showing.
I'm taking off these designer's pant suits...
They cost too much...to smell like...
Broccoli soup!...
I'm putting on my blue jeans...
And big shirts...
With two seams...
And then look, real mean...
Like the modern moms...going to a Ghetto prom...

Yeah...throw on some fake braids or curly wig...
Going out to do a jig...not do a 'Gig'...

Throw on a frown...that says...this child has to go...
Cause I'm going to get down (for me...
Down...is in the bed...resting my head...
From the heavy load) pearly whites don't show any more...
Shoot out their lips...
Let'em quiver and be a little stiff...
Looking at TV...and listening to some bad rap...
Gives them a bit of a lift. Now, these diversions don't fit under...
my cap...
I'd rather take me a nap!!

I figure that I am betwixt and between...
A young modern and an antique form...fusing the old with the
new...which blends into...a unique mom

I thank God that I am so blessed...even though, somewhat
stressed...with the Compulsory educational studies...(homework)
that I had forgotten...since my...Thirties.

I can still shoot a ball in a basket...
And not feel that I am ready...
For a casket...
Yea-hey...very much alive...
I'm gonna keep this feeling...until I am
At least–sixty-five!!
Teaching and preaching–doctoring
Colds and wiping noses...
Tending injured knees and itchy hives...
With sympathy and a...compassionate smile.

Sometimes...I call on the Lord...and I cry out...
"Lord help your chile !!

Both of us!...energy...plus
It's a must.
Show your face...help me to run this race...
And win this case...
My charge...that you gave to me...truly encompass my heart...
And the duties are...not too hard...
But, from you...my God...
I am in need...of a merciful and...
Sympathetic nod.
The age factor was not deemed...
When my assignment...came into being...it seems...
And I sense, that it's more about.
Building character...of high spiritual esteem.
I'm not necessarily, too ole! You see...
But, I do need you...to cover me...
With your love and tender mercies...

So, please, hear my petitions...and pleas...while, I bow down
On...my knees!!

WOMEN OF THE NEW MILLENNIUM

We are at this point and time...
Ready to go another round...
As we enter into a new era...
Women...will, now, be crowned...
In the wake of...a new millennium.
We have fought...scratched and scream
Every step of the way...
It seems...
Dregs from the bitter cup...we have sipped...
Of first rate citizenship.

We laid and played...slipped our
Hips and pushed out pouting lips...
Finally, realizing...that we have been...
duped and gypped...
Acquiring only a previous few...
Of the computer chips.
So, our achievement is, still, nil...
With some desires and dreams...
Yet to be fulfill.

The government represented itself...as a friend...
If our subsistence...on it we depend...
Requiring us to oust...and hide our men...
Leaving us lonely...longing and alone...

To nourish and fend...
For...our chil-dren.

The system succeeded in cracking...
The family code...and bulldozed us...
into an insidious role...
Of being 'the head of household'...
Forcing us to bear the burden...
Of this heavy and...
Unfair load.

Meager subsidies...in dispersion...
Allotted to us...with condescension.
Now, we have the distinction...of being...
"The welfare recipi--yents!"
Though, the aid is given...trying to appease...
It is offered in contempt...assuming that...we would
be pleased.
There is nothing to decide...and where is pride??
When we're forced to depend...on that...so called friend!

Well by now...we have learned to accept...
Without chagrin...a penurious check;
A stipend...the purchase price for our self-respect.
The wedge was shrewdly place...
Between families...to divide and separate...
So subtle...as it disguises...
The offensive and...monstrous fate.

Procedures were used to keep...control...
While we mortgage our weary...souls...
Yielding to vicious ridicule...
Of being on the welfare...payrolls.

The cruel mockery...inevitably...
Took its dastardly toll.

The beast that rode it's victims...is, now, being ridden.
As the future looms with...doom for the masses of 'created'
de-pendent...classes.
The system is consumed with fear...
Cause the 'brainchild' has bought...into the same idea...
To make it big business...a profit gain...not a...
poverty pain...
But the differences is..."big g" pays the cost...
For "brainchild" to be the boss!...it's called,
'Admini-stra-tive...loss!!

While the welfare muddle...accelerates...
The family unit dwindles...and disintegrates.
The government, now, is busy...using it's clout...
To kick the recipients off...of welfare and out...
Into a labor force...that they know nothing...about.

The people are saying..."How are we to survive?...
We have been taken care of...for generations...
Even all of our lives!
The big question is...as we contemplate...
What is the fate...of our welfare states?

Assuredly, the problematic and programmatic public
as-sis-tance...
Has not plan...to well...in advance.
Dependents were encouraged...
To rely and die...in the arms of its political...
and plotted schemes...

While promising to assist...with their hopes and dreams.
This created a life-line hinge...to the system of a...
bureaucratic fringe.
The recipients are expected, now, to wing-it...
On wings that...
Are impinged and singed.

Warning! Warning! Another strategic plot...
Brewing and simmering...in the pot!
The order and structure of previous things...
Like a pendulum...begins to swing...
And will soon come to a haltering...stop.

Where do we go from here?
How will we merge into...
The new millennium...?
With a humming song...by the beat of...a drum?
Or...will we flood...
Into the new century...
As a roaring surge of...women...
With voices raised...in unison...like a mighty rush of
ocean waves...
Being joyful seekers...and future keepers?

Too, long...our minds have been used in areas
behind the scenes...
Because 'knowing' is in our genes.
How then...can we speak...
But mustn't be seen?
It is imperative...that we ascend...
From the position of complacency and go forth...
gracefully...

Presenting our personal platform...
On women issues...
While, bearing up to ugly...and aggressive misuse.

We must defend our rights...
To...be!!!
Heirs on earth...as in heaven
Because we are partners in a...joint tena-cy
Whether we are male or female...
To God...it is irrelevant!

He designated our roles...to be a "help-meet";
So, why continue to rule the world...
Behind closed doors...and between two sheets...
Being exploited like wenches...
inhabiting the streets??

Sh!-sh!- sh! While they are being...trained...
Our technique...must be discreet.
We're granting our brains...to be drained...
(you see)
Giving our best...to receive less...
Boosting their egos...to be our conquering heroes.
Thereby, positioning...ourselves...
as their first conquest.

However, our intellect should be noted...
as being
Above and beyond...the traditional maneuver
of a feel-good...masseur
We were formed and calibrated...
In the 'Garden of Eden's' college...

And flowing thru us...is the motherlode of creative knowledge!
Wake up! We are the warden...and don't need to be pardon!
I know that it has been over-emphasized...that...
we are the weaker sex...
But this only applies...
to the physical aspect...
And doesn't explore...the brilliance of...
Our mental crest.
Henceforth...our aspirations...will not be
Misconceived...and our purposes will be...achieved!!

In the commencement...of this millennium
We will take steps...from behind...and
underneath...the man.
Yes! It's time to take a stand...
Upward...not downward...for our own destiny...
we are accountable!

Women of the new millennium!...come!!
Let's join hands...as sisters...and form a band of understanding...
Whatever the color...race...or...circumstances...
Closing out the evil forces of jealousy...hostility...
and hate!!!
And use the key of 'Unity and love'...
to blast open the urbanomic's gate!!!

We will allow our experiences and wisdom...
gained in the past...
Be used as a bridge...that has prepared us...
For our future tasks.
Let then be a soaring power within...
Lifting us to higher heights...thus, wielding them as our...
guiding lights.

We will share spiritual, intellectual, and physical
strengths...
Merge resources...and change history...as we move
towards new courses...
Establishing goals and objectives...permitting our bonds of...
love and respect...to be entrenched.
Women!!! --- of the new mil-len-nium!!! We will march
To our own drum beat...
Discarding old attitudes of defeat...unloading the filthy
baggage...of drugs...
And purging the evil...
That it serves!

Even though...our self esteem has been brought...
Low...
And scraped to the very...core...
We will pull up...by our lacey bootstrap...
Detaching...the gender...
Booby trap.

Let's look to God for our...guidance...
We are his assorted spices...of life...in us He abides...
And in Him...we must confide
As we flow with our times...of the tides...

We'll embrace new ideas and
Encourage...various...opinions...
That will display the new image...
Of bonding age, race and creed.
We are a new breed...on this pilgrimage...
Persisting in the pursuit of women privileges...
while performing incredible deeds...
In our demands to be freed!!

No matter...what colors are in...the family tree...
We all have responsibilities...and special-ties...
Enough to make an impressive...impact...
When we march...though, furiously attacked...
into the new millennium.

Let's praise God...in loud exaltations!!!
And leave behind...daily sobbing...
of yesteryear's horrors...
We'll join together...in a new start...uniting with love...
In our hearts.
The glow of grand expectations; helps us to face the
gleaming tomorrows;
As we rise above...the suffering and sorrows.

We will...emanate excellence and notable presence...
with excited trembling...
While marching into the new millennium.
Our well earned laurels...
And just rewards...beckon to us...
Women!!! WOMEN of the millennium!!!

TOUCH UPON

Each day of our lives,
We are touched upon...
By someone;
Who makes this life
Special and worthwhile.

We, sometimes; recognize them,
Immediately.
Oft times, they pass
Fleetingly;
Before we know that the role
They play,
Holds special meanings
To help us...
As we travel...along...the way.

Oh! How we should, then, capture and extract...
From each word, smile and act,
The love, that comes from this human impact;
Realizing, one simple fact ---
That they may never pass us again,
On the way back!

We are somehow strengthen
With the knowledge;

When our Pastor, Overseer Streeter,
Practiced this logic...
And stopped and pause with us one day,
To touch us lovingly
On the way!

THE AMAZING GRACE

The "Word" was limply draped
Upon the cross...
The moment was consecrated...
As he concentrated,
On dedicating his life...to redeem the loss.
This...was an hour for us to rejoice...
For before the foundation...
He had made...the choice.

He hung there for you and me upon the bloody tree...

He hung there...
For those of us, who were in despair...

He hung there for the cowards...
who thought that they had the power...
While, humbly, he hung there!

They gaped and gazed...
At the amazing grace,
As the blood ran down
Thru the thorny crown...
... and...
Oozed into his face...
From his sides...came blood and water...

That splashed upon his dripping feet!

And the sounds were intertwined with the crowd's...
boisterous laughter!!
Nevertheless, he couldn't retreat...in defeat...
because the cross...he chose to bear so,...he hung there!

The people were appalled...as they formed a human wall;
And gathered at the bottom of the hill...of Golgatha

It was a bit of a chill...and very still...
While they witnessed the death of...the greatest life...
that ever lived!
He was the "finisher and the author"!
And never wavered...as he held them up in prayer...
While he hung there!

Finally, he cried out...with a thundering shout:
"Father, forgive them!"...
And they watched...in guilty shock...
While his spirit left...it's earthly realm...
His body dangled...from the sacrificial limb...
A living testimony...that he cared...
Because he hung in there!!

The good news is this: we were saved from a dastardly abyss...
As his blood flowed...we were transfused...
transformed...and restored.
When he was resurrected...we were given eternal shelter...
Under his hold scepter...and...
Thru his grace...we were embraced...

Perfected and protected...recognized and crystallized with the
eternal love of our Father...and the blood of the lamb...
"The Amazing Grace" and "The Living Water"
They are the "Alpha...and Omega"!

H. Davison
September 18, 1998
Revised October 24, 1998

SARAH
A DEDICATION TO GRANDPARENTS

The Lord visited Sarah in her old age...
"You'll bring forth a child...in a short while",...
She heard and was...amazed..."How so..., I just turned
Ninety...about a year ago ,,, everything now...is numb, wrinkled
and...shriveled..."
At this musing, she began to...giggle...
"Why do you laugh? Said the Lord, "The plans are...recorded.
He is the promised seed of many nations...
for an everlasting...duration'.
Even though...Sarah was astonished...
As she was admonished...
She couldn't keep...nor hold back...the mirth that...seeped...
like water under pressure...it creeped...
As she thought of them having...pleasure...hah...hah...and a
gleeful...
Hee–hee!...OO...ho!--ho!...ho!

Then she said,..."We have waxed too old!
Too many years...have put us...in a rickety mold"...
Well, she had forgotten the power of God...
Although the job must have been...mighty hard...
as he took her old body...began to remake and reshape...
tightening muscles...in all the appropriate places...

Reopening channels...that had been closed...for ages...
Putting zip and pep...in her feeble step...
Her eyes began to sparkle...and her fussing turn to...
laughter...
She was ready to have some fun!!!... And more...fun!!!–
Of course Abraham...too, had things...redone...
He began to rise for the special occasion...
Didn't have to wait for the usual...persuasion...
He could stand on an...implied command...made him feel...
like a brand new man!...
He told Sarah..."The time has been...long...
Since, I've felt so...strong!!
Hush! I feel a rush...let's get my nations 'Going on!!'
Well, the Lord blessed her with the 'Pleasure...'of conceiving
the...promised seed...
And gave us (grandmas) our inheritance...so we could help...
feed...
All the [ly] areas that the little critters...
Have needs...[physical-ly, mental-ly, emotional-ly and
spiritual-ly]
'Caused they're our treasures...
And absolute-ly our planted seeds!! ----------

STOP THE VIOLENCE

Yo ho! Yo Ho!
Stop the violence...no need to fight
Using brain power...shows your might
Leaving the gangs...is your natural rights!!
Don't cave in...and don't you crash...
Make a quick dash...you ain't no coward...just...
Stop the violence! Stop the violence!

Yo ho! Yo ho!
Put down your guns...let's have some fun!
How can you learn...when you're on the run?
Head exploding...while bullets churn?
Unless you want to be...a shroud of silence...
Stop the violence! ... Stop the violence!

Yo ho! Yo ho!
Bind your devils...rise to a new level
Destroy your swords...break your knives
It'll help save...children's lives...
And quit being dense...don't straddle the fence...
Stop the violence! Stop the violence!

Yo ho! Yo ho!
There's no straight way...you'll have to pay...
"Don't fear these choices!"...I hear you say...

'Til your body is twisted...like an old coat rack...
Needing someone...to put you in the 'sack'...
Hey! Your life will never be the same!...
Cause- you- hung out...with the wrong wolf
gang...Destroyed your family...and their precious
name...Where is your gang? Where is your
gang??

None of this...makes good sense...use your
Intelli-gence...
Stop the violence! Stop the violence!

Yo ho! Yo ho!
You choose...to live behind- big- black bars...
Never seeing the moon...nor the shining stars...
Cause your head is hard...like a steel jack
Hammer...you'll spend your life...in a dark cold
slammer.
Maybe, when...enough is said...you will be...
somewhat convinced...to
Stop the violence! Stop the violence!

Yo ho! Yo ho!
Put down your pipe...and all other- drug types...
Causing confusion- as you embrace delusions...
Your parents crying...people are gawking...
You in darkness...of your plush...velvet coffin...
Your life is en-ded!...as a hawker and stalker...
Your parents are not laughing...while they play
the violin...
Be real! Here is the deal! Move away from

where you've been! Don't use your life...being
offensive...
Get smart...and get defensive...
Spread the alarm...don't be leery...and drop your
Ar-till-ery!!!

**Stop the violence! Stop the violence! Stop the
violence!** Stop the violence!

THE LYING BEAST

Well...we have gone and done it;
We have allowed the 'powers that be'...
To enter therein...
Using a guise so subtle...
that our eyes couldn't see...
There they were...big as sin...
Binding up the minds...of our chil-dren!!
We were told about the new procedure...
reading without phonetics...
That paved the way for the...controversial
teaching...of phonic-e-bonics...
What is this?? Don't ask me...but-t-t...I am
wary...when it's not found...in Webster's
Diction-ary!!
We're told...that the basic sounds
Of' ABC's'...is not necessary...to spell and read.
The modern thing is ...just read the pictures...
Like the cave men did...in the era of...
Hieroglyphics!
Yes, we parents stood by...and quietly permitted it!
Now!!! Since...the child can't spell nor read...
Listen to the Euphonics...of 'modern' Pedantics,...
Prancing around...like little penguins...
Trying to revolutionize...perfect Englist...
Into a new dia-lect...

Articulating, that "we need an Ebonic...text"...
To teach grammer;
Making it coincide...with the bureaucratic lie...
That our children can only learn...in this
prehistoric manner...

"Cause dey kan't be taut to tawk...good Anglesh...
wid'ot it–neder!!
And- we will go another step, further,...to
emotional-ly disturb your seed...we won't let you
worship God...in schools,...nor quote by memo-
ry...the Golden Rules." Hey!! We stood by like
powerless dolts...while they pressed their laws
in legislative courts!

The 'system' forces...gains control...by
brainwashing our children...as it steals their souls...
Teaching them...that they're misused and
abused...it says, "lean on my many tentacles...and depend...
Just trust me...as a caring friend...cause
Your parents are really...the en-e-mies!"...
So, tell me...how can our mouths...
Be shut tight...against such extremities...
is it because...we think it's right???

So these glorious globs of our flesh...are
translated and pitched...into the arena of a
systematic...mess...as we watch in a trance...and acquiesce.
Jesus, as our Lord...is restricted knowledge...
Methods are used...which he is slowly being...abolish!!!
Leaving our children's minds...null and void...
While their psyche incompetence...
Surpasses the analysis of Sigmund Freud.

Meantime...papa 'govern...and momma 'ment...
move in and demolish...whatever moral virtue...
that our children have left.

They enclose their iron-clad fist...around their
hard heads and stiff little necks...
Then...squeeze-e-e...accelerating moral decay...
and assured death!!...
The price we parents...and children pay...
By keeping quiet...and playing deaf.

We have opened wide!!!...the doors...for
the 'faux parents' to walk in...like border patrols...
to take over...what God gave to us. Who is going
to defend? I –tell-you-this!...He is the one...
that we must trust! We are not generics...in an
abyss...we are the original and the first!!!
Of course our–parental authority...is being
challenged...but it is essential...for us to rally...
replacing shame with dignity...
As we are thoroughly maneuvered...and perused...
without privity.

The welfare program no longer needs...to have our consent!!!
Cause, now, the bones of our bones...are trained...
and their minds are twisted and bent...made to
feel like...they're all alone...and free...to make a
choice...cause the system...will readily agree...
that they are treated wrong!!
"Diss'n" them ---is a no-no!!...behind the bars...

you will go!! And to the judge...the keys are
thrown...while the wheels of justice...
moves...very slow!!!

Overnite...where are the children?...The little
buggers are acting like they're grown!...Being
baby parents...still living in the home!!! We are
commanded by...them and --- 'them'...to take care
of their needs...clothes and feed...
Even, while being retained...'behind bars'...of
steel I maintain...we are parents, have been...
"diss'n!" and this whole hideous thing...has
gone too far!!
Know ye! Know ye!...and listen! We, are hard
repressed...to rear and discipline...our blood and
flesh...and are being compelled to omit...the laws
of God's holy 'Word'. Consequently, we are
losing...our self-respect and the children's high
esteem...for us!

The generics, acting as authorities...take control
and wrench our children from our arms...they are
then...caught up into the system...as political pawns...
What is the outcome...for the suffering of...
parents and children...???
Low self-esteem and inferiorities!!!...
Who cares about our loving hearts...being thrown
into psychological shock .,..
As they are torn from their homes???...
The system??...hum-m-m...I think-not!
But, we can see a traditional symbolism...a subtle
stratagem...that has a familiar resemblance...

To the era of the...slavery cataclysm.
It is indicative that this slave mentality...still
exists and uses the same pattern...like a black
shadow...swooping down...
On any race...at any given time...or place.
There is something about this picture...that's
wrong. It is time to bring order...and be strong...
And take charge of our own children and...home!!

However, conditions must not be created...
For them to be taken...neither, should we condone...
them being forsaken.
Admittedly, a dysfunctional home can be on either
side of the door...
Own home or the other home...some good...
some to be abhorred...
Facing danger and deception...on either end...of
the right and wrong...spectrum! But, the system
thinks that the problems are being resolved, while
moving them about...in and out...of a foster
home...the welfare "Sorority" house!!

With our minds and hands tied and bound up in
Fears...we are, now, drowning in helpless tears...,
We can no longer hug the little 'dears'...the
system frowns upon it...as a possible molestation
case...
So, we live in a constant atmosphere of dread...
and frustration.
We can no longer paddle their little 'hindies'...
Just anticipating the visit of poppa 'govern' and
moma 'ment'...renders us helpless and...spineless.

They readily accuse us...of child abuse...and
don't seek proof nor the truth...
Only the nearest 'caboose!' ---
Then, the family relationships are broken and
restrained...
A bond...that can never be the same...

Now, that the parents of the system...are in full
control...they implement much stronger goals...
Causing our children minds...to pivot...
While being reduced...to stupid little idiots...
So, that they'll do whatever...is being taught and
told.
They have become immuned to pain...
while being trained...and instilled...to go out and kill...
kill!! Kill!!

I hear the pseudo-parents say, 'I have mesmerized
you...through your television sets...filled with
filth...violence and sex!!!
I enchanted you in the movies...and through your
videos and radios...you were hypnotized...
I am speaking and teaching rebellion...
And disrespect...and that your parents...
Are prime suspects...
Therefore you must reject!!!
Henceforth, your brains have been fully
captured...and now your soul...
can be our dispatcher.
We are your gods...worship us...I gave you blood
To drank...and filthiest of filth to eat...
Your death and others...have me to 'thank'.

I blow your brains out, first...with drugs.
Spankings and beatings...you take from me!!!
I rip your hearts out in gang wars...
Now, you can see...
That you are a real tough thug...
Fighting for my cause.
Discipline from your parents...you report.
You only need them...for your financial
support!...your ugliness will come up to me as my
sweet smelling… fetor...cause you are my
cheaters..."

While your parents sit by listless and powerless...
let **me**...your psychologist, psychiatrist, social
service welfare...and schools as I pretend to care...

Take over what rightfully belong to them...while I
share in the custody...as parent pro-tem...
And I will abolish God...to make their parenting
job...real hard!!!
Finally, you are ready for me!...I will take my
bazookas and machine guns...
Just for fun...and blast your buttocks...up into
the sun...
Around the clock...and over every city block!

Parents...be secured in the knowledge...the
children has no control...in a world that's so
sordid...
We left the doors wide open for the beast...
So he sneaked in and stole...while, we were busy
setting...our financial goals.

Our children were made to be the last and least...
Now, the monster is fat...from devouring their
innocent meat...yet in horror, we permit...and
submit to ignominious...defeat.

Get up parents!!...get up now!!!
We will not stand by and be dormant...
Strength...must be found!...we must fight...and
get our children back!!
Taking the first step...back to God's guidance...
on that...there is no...deciding!
He is our only hope.

We must stop their conniving...and confront these
serious issues...that have been misconstrued...or
we will join our children to be consumed...
in a big fat feast...for this monstrous...and greedy
beast!!!

THE ORIGIN OF THE PHOENIX

At some point in time; I had read about this mystical bird–and the legend goes—as death nears, the Phoenix begins to prepare a nest of aromatic boughs and spices; then after the completion–it sets the Pyre on fire and is consumed there in the flames...subsequently, rising miraculously; from the ashes as a reborn Phoenix.

The phoenix, described in Literature had its home near the rising sun...normally in Arabia or India, where spices were plentiful for the Pyre. The coloring of the Phoenix...its connection with fire and supernatural rebirth; along with other features of the Fable, are allegorical of the sun itself with its promise of dawn after sunset–and life after death.

I was enchanted with this bird's ability to come back to "Ground Zero" and burn itself up–just to start all over again. Howbeit, **if anyone...or anything** traveled for hundreds of years; [**I** surmise] would have embedded in all of its body parts–a collection of Antediluvian debris and residue -- inevitably, **becoming one with it**. In any event; this could explain the reason for the necessitation of the Phoenix's incineration [**Wye–of course...that's it!!**] This was the only **logical** way to free itself! Hu-mn!...this is a provocative thought, wouldn't you think?

However, the Phoenix's eyes were upon the prize of rising again as a brand new creature...after dumping all of its encumbrances of filthiness and dirt; **discouragements...obstacles...barriers...hindrances... obstructions** of all kinds...and all other **oppressive forces** -- upon the Pyre of the flaming fire.

We, today, would do well to follow this example...Oh No! **not the fire** made by hands...but the **Holy Ghost Fire**–made by His Spirit!...

and when we submit our evil, wicked and sinful ways–upon **His Pyre**...
then Jesus can 'create a clean heart...and renew a right spirit within us–so
that we become reborned creatures, to "Press towards the mark for the
prized"...while daily living under the shadow of God's hand!

It is rewarding to be at peace, when the world is blowing its brains
out...with an influx of evil morbidity. However...to find this solace; we
must let the Holy Spirit take control of our lives and lead us into the
power of Jesus' love. Then...**and only then**...can the new creature keep
renewing himself by throwing off; the filthy rags of...**emotional pain,
financial lack, worries over the children**...who have gone "Hog wild
and country crazy" [An old saying that just came back to memory]...and
even to the ugly behavior of husbands and wives, who act like "God's
loose mules!" [excuse me, another aphorism popped out!]

We must cast off the scatological < I like this word > [filth...obscene...
excremental] rags of **hate...jealousy...hostility...ugly attitudes and all
of the other 'scats!**'...**AND** put them right on Jesus' shoulders...yea'–
even in his lap, as we rest under the wings of the Holy Spirit.

Now...since we have unloaded our burdens–I feel free with this new-
ness and peace!!! What about you??? **YES! A refreshing freedom**–which
is analogous to the **RISING OF A REBIRTHED** Phoenix.

THE PHOENIX

The beautiful Phoenix builds his nest...upon a pyre so that its body burns in the blazing fire...and out of its ashes–rises–reborn–renewed...and full of energies–facing the sun with fresh beginnings...[some say...a life that spans from 500 to 1000 years–before the next death reappears.] Then back to the burning pyre–firey ashes–and graceful risings–to launch another brand new creature into the horizon. A somewhat symbolism of life and demise–but the difference is– man's body deteriorates there in the dirt–while the soul transforms into rebirth–as it leaves the earth–and commutes to the great beyond–to wait for its destiny and fate.

The Phoenix rises from his smoldering ashes–with plumage all-aglow...as the open wings display brilliancy of bright scarlet and shimmering gold–then it, slowly, begins to soar–effort-less-ly–floating into the air...leaving the ashes of death–and hopeless despair.

The Legend of the Phoenix's extermination and the rising from his ashes–are metaphors of mankind's degradation–and, also, the necessity for procedural elimination. The question is–what is a better place than upon the Holy Ghost-Pyre?

Throw in some of these splinters for kindling...in his purging...fire. Discard cheating and deceitful actions–lying and stealing clashes–backbiting and peace smashing...and a lot of other trash -- let them all cremate into smithereens of ashes–and after this transformation into righteousness–rise and claim spiritual rebirth in meekness–while inheriting the earth–and in the midst of joy–put on glorious wings–to fly all over the Heavens–to see our Lord Jesus...and finally,–standing before the awesome Father-God–in sacred...reverence.

The allegory of Moses captures a period of political upheaval...and the trials in his life...were inconceivable...it was during this time...that God intervened...with the burning bush scene. He immediately began to...snatch off his dirty patches...slinging them upon the...flaming pyre... and the very first one–was 'submission and obedience'...that went into the fire "take off your shoes, Moses!" As he moved with expedience... transfusing spiritual ...ingredients. First...he began to take off the old garments...that had been his biggest torment...; rejections and depressions...debasing and humiliations...defeatism and low self-esteem... there were others...also redeemed...he plucked him like a chicken... leaving nothing for pickings...as he quietly and methodically...dumped them...one by one...into the burning fire...

All the while, as God patiently taught him faith...Moses squirmed in his ashes...gasping from these actions, saying, "but Lord, I am slow in speech" [paraphrasing] "Why, even my tongue is too slow to chew...so what do I do...what do I say to them??– and God just calmly turned the fire upon him–I can hear him say...'enough already'!!– I'm not listening to any more of Moses'..."Buts!!"

Soon the distrust that he had in God and himself...were burned in the flames of mystical death...and his pessimisms became smashes of sooty...ashes...which God transformed into a divine creature...A supernatural preacher!

Well Moses was energized...and with special strength in his spiritual wings...he, frequently, waved them...and like the Phoenix...he was brand new and was clear on everything...nothing was dim. Now, he could flap himself right out of his comfort zone–of non-committal... even quitting his mental and emotional fiddling–! He was ready for the flight...anxious to demonstrate God's–might. **Yeah! Yeah! A new walk! Espousing a new talk!** Willing and ready to work for the cause [I can just hear him say] **Now! Now! Let's me and you...God–lay down some laws...gotta be some changes of heart–round heah!...We're gonna**

get your stiff necked 'chillin' straight or we are kicking 'em right outa the gate. Hunh–Lord? Isn't this a familiar trait...when, we Christians, begin to go straight?

Howbeit, a drastic change takes place...when short comings are thrown upon Pyre...of the Holy Ghost Fire...a fire that no one can put out–as we proceed to spread it around—and all about!...

Of course–all will not receive...as this prophet had perceived... Elijah, a mighty prophet, among prophet–whose praying could stop the rain–and order it back again. He spoke and hundreds in the lots of fifty–dropped dead...and his fame reached a woman whose son had died. He, simply, stretched himself on the child three times and prayed...and God brought the boy back -- alive.

Nevertheless, he didn't feel his best–because the children of Israel was giving him–stress. They were bowing their knees down to Baal and kissing him on his lips–hands and fingertips.

"All of 'em God! with the exception of me"–he wailed.

Not so Elijah! I have reserved, for me, seven-thousands–Now, call four hundred and fifty of Baal's prophets...into the desert island. A bullock is to be prepared on both sides –for a day's sacrifice–to test and see which god starts–the fire.

Baal's prophets got busy –preparing the alter and praying that their god–would surely listen. Meantime, Elijah was on the upper level– taunting–teasing–jeering and reveling–while they pouted and began doubting...cutting themselves with weapons... hoping their god would fire up any second. They jumped up and down on the altar – blood pouring from their chests–gushing on the Bul-lock–wood and rocks –indeed a bloody mess! Needless to say...their faith faltered –after their god had failed the –test !!!

Subsequent to this grand stand fracas –Elijah prepared his alter. It was well past mid-day and a lot of time had to be taken.

The bullock...wood...and rocks...on the alter...had to be placed just so...and drenched. The water over flowed as they poured–and like a river–it ran in the dugout trench. When this was finished–Elijah did not flinch–he just began to pray. Suddenly! God's fire came down from Heaven and consumed the bullock –there in the evening of the day... and the alter of wood–where it stood–the twelve stones–representing the twelve tribes of Israel –were all gone...and with a gusty wind the dust went...then after this spiritual sup...all of the water was lapped up!!

Well Jezebel owned these profane prophets and after the confrontation of..."Big Who and the Little You"...justice was not due –And following God's order–Elijah demanded that they be caught and brought to the Brook of Ki-Shon...hence, the bloody show was on...they were bowed and cowered...all four hundred and fifty...more than a few–that Elijah slew. There is no doubt –he felt the rush of control and power– as he was chopping off four hundred and fifty loathsome heads–and thought that he had it made...until . ---..

Jezebel wrote him an "I'm gonna get you note"...it's amazing how quickly the miracles that he had wrought–thru the spirit and power of God–he'd forgotten!! It's no different–today–when our faith is a challenge and hard trials that we face–gives way to fear and doubting! Well, Elijah became so frightened–he began running for his life...as if he was hiding out-- from a wife...and after he took refuge under the juniper tree–'he began his plea..."Oh!–Lord...just let me die...I am not better than my father!" Interpretation" ['I, too, am full of pride–I, too, am subject to fear–I, too engage–in bloodletting and fretting–I, too am not perfect–I, too, am vain–and–arrogant...now–I am ashamed'] "Oh! I've had enough Lord, I don't want to be alive!" [paraphrasing] take me now–that I fall not in the hands of Jezebel–and be put thru her living hell!

Well...the Lord comforted him–like a small child...sending him back to complete his mission...and to prepare him for his exit–in style. God told Elijah to 'anoint Elisha to be the prophet in his room'–here on earth...because he was to travel the rest of the way–as a rebirth.

Then one day–walking along with Elisha–there was a roaring and rushing sound–that was going around and zooming down...seemingly, quite a distance–afar. Then suddenly!–The whirlwind–divided them apart and swooped Elijah into the blazing chariot–driven by horses–making strange noises–like chirps of parrots–while carrying him into the heavenly garrets.

Now, here is a mystery, not a biblical theory–merely a supposition–perhaps fictional–but for a moment–let's peer at this picture–what if–at that precise moment–there was no sound of the trumpet–or any other noise–it was fairly quiet–the only thing heard–was the crackling of fire... and his body being consumed on the–burning pyre. But he leaves his ashes...after his soul detaches–as he quickens in spiritual union...with the flaming carriage...whirling into the universe in the similitude of a marriage.

Now...the reborn Phoenix with floating wings–glides into the sun–until it's time for him to come back and be redone–but Elijah's spirit soared into the heavens and never again–would return to earth for repetitive–rebirths. [However, there is a mystery when Jesus said of John the Baptist that "Elias is indeed come" and he that hath ears to hear...let him hear"–Malachi 4:5, Matthew 11:14 and Mark 9:13]

But the birth of births–were Jesus Christ–who walked on the earth–with a man's footprints...teaching and preaching in the spirit of God;–from whence He was sent–and for our souls–he paid the price–even for the wicked and–evil heart.

He was born into the world to teach us how to live–and for him to die that we may be saved and have eternal life. He took no sins of His own to his **wooden pyre–He** only took our filthy rags–purging them in **His love**...making them bright and clean thru his **sacrificial–blood**... and while he was **being crucified**–we were transformed–from **hopeless sinful–ashes**...and purified in the Holy Ghost–fire–rising with him–floating on the wings of faith–anticipation and hope...becoming new creatures of an immortal–life.

After Jesus was entombed–who knows how long he stayed in his shroud–after the silence of the jeering–crowd? But one thing is ascertain–He had further work after his terrible pain there on the cross... because other souls–already buried in the earth–were, also, lost and patiently waiting...their rebirth.

With **three days**–and a lot to say...there was no time to **rest**–he had to rush to **get re-dress**...and the Holy Spirit ignited the **fire of power**–for him to **rise from his pyre**...within the very **same hour**. He **snatched** the bloody clothes off–rising above the death of–**ashes** and **distractions**–with **eyes flashing**–went into the **hearth of the earth**–to **teach–preach** and **beseech**.

His messages were so powerful–that the graves couldn't hold the **saints**–who burst forth and **hit the streets**! [My thinking is] some of the living–**fainted** and other standbys–looked for **extra feet**!

Finally...he had completed all errands that the Father had sent him on...Now, it was time to be reborn–for his Heavenly home...but this time as the sovereign–king–ready to take his throne. And He rose!... with glory–strength and dominion!! Hallelujah!!!!–He rose!!

Seemingly, I hear the Father boast...[as we do when our children excel] while looking over at the–Holy Ghost...'that's my son...I want you to take Gabri-el and the Angels–yes, the whole host–to escort Him back here –to be at my right side'...Well!! They all came with floating and fluttering wings –gathering around Jesus and began to sing –slowly, ascending with him into the Heavens–for His eternal–reign.

Heretofore, the dying of the mystical Phoenix on his firey pyre –and the renewing thru his burning ashes –did not rise to eternal life...nor was there a price exacted –or lives impacted –for his continual deaths and risings. There is no kingdom built in His name–or sufferings for the world–while enduring pain. It appears that His only contribution was the mystique to die–and arise as a creature of magnificent beauty–which is not conductive to an everlasting life...and his only validity–of living– was in the mysticism and spiritualism–of someone's mind.

Our Lord and Savior had one death–and only one pyre–the Cross–and our lives continue to be directed by his choice of birth–death and resurrection–and is forever–our Spiritual Nucleus–of hope–that dictates our fate–and by dying–he paid the price to validate mortals, transforming them into immortals–for God's purposes.

When our transgressions were burned in the ashes–on Jesus' pyre –by the divine power and Holy Ghost fire…He rose with our redemption in his hand–a completed phase of his plan. Our lives–then–were transformed into a rebirth–making us new creatures–to live on earth. He was a living sacrifice–for all people. He is our God, the Son…our Savior… and our supernatural keeper!!!

FOREWORD
BROTHER'S KEEPER

W hen my friend, Barbara Charles, ask me to do a poetry narration for the NAACP's Luncheon...I said, "Oh my goodness the mover and shaker is at it again!" But how could I say, "NO" when I have been commissioned by Father-God??? The poetry is not mine to withhold...But to share!

This piece of poetry was composed after searching the spirit for a proper subject matter. The Holy Spirit brought to mind, some of the Biblical Brothers...and I thought. "This is great and, also, in apropos to some of the principles of the NAACP that follow the lines of encouragement–of coming together–and the advancement of a people."

How many of us believe that we should be each other's keepers? **And even to the least desirable–we must love one another. Jesus said in St. Matthew, Chapter 5:4 "For if ye love them which love you, what rewards have ye? Do not even the publicans the same? And if ye salute your brethren only, what do you more than others? Do not even the publicans, so?"**

This gave leeway to some deep thought on my part–and I started thinking...It's awfully hard to love someone; who has done you a dirty! And frankly speaking–**I cannot**!! So I ask Jesus to love them through me! **But oh?** What **sweet peace and bliss**, when we can throw the hate and hostility over on the shoulder of the Lord!

Can we answer in the affirmative; when asked to do good things for others? Now this is easy to do–if we like the person–or, if we feel

that a person is good!!...But what about the **low-down dirty uglies??**...
Now!!–we have a real problem with this one! **Remember**–Jesus has
said–even sinners can love the good ones!

But–until–we are spiritually conditioned–Our fingers are **turned
into a pointer**–and our **tongues** are like a poisonous Asp–hissing [small
poisonous snake] **animosity–enmity–malice and antagonism!!** We
begin to stew and spew...'forget that!!! They did me a dirty!...**so now–
this** ...They're gonna **get right back!!!**...and most likely–we'll succumb
to the '**tit for tat**' retaliation...asking the age old question...why should I
treat them any better --- **Am I my Brother's Keeper???** ---

AM I MY BROTHER'S KEEPER

Am I my brother's keeper?
Why should I **sow good seeds–to cause him to be a good reaper**?
Must I share my home and land–to just any man?
Well,–whether I am of **color**–or-- no color ... **Wye[Y]**...I'll **just**
move in --and take from you–**and** my other brother.
Cain first ask this question...when his brother–he had slain...He felt it
was for justice–because his **sacrifice was vain**...
the earth was crusty–where **Abel had been lain**...
The blood had **oozed out–pointing to his whereabouts**!...
God thundered–**Where is your brother, Cain?**
His **blood cries out to me...over there underneath the tree!**
Well–Cain must have felt very guilty...and terrible–**ashamed!**

B ut being a cold-blooded murderer–he did not stutter...somewhat indignant–while talking smack! Even thought...he was the one... caught in the ungodly act!...A common practice for all...when on the carpet–we are called!!

As he blurted loudly...I hear him say...[**and I paraphrase**] **How do I know–I don't keep him by my side–to watch over him–like he's my child**...and as God frowned–his troubles got deeper–and with **head hung down-he said sheepishly..."Am I My Brother's Keeper?"**

We see Jacob and Esau–**classic sibling rivalry**...beginning with **Esau's stomach growling–and ending with him whopping and howling–When he traded his birthright–for a bowl of soup.** But after he **got full**; he **wanted to fight**...making a charge of an unduly–right! However...each one connived --- and to evil–they both stoop!

95

But...**Esau had the gall...to make a call to their father–while his belly was bulging from his brother's–pottage and water**...He was **ready to break his contract–or the neck of Jacob**...and now, he was out and his twin was --- in!...There was nothing his father could do–cause the deed was done; his life's course would have to make the full–run.

And now...since he's the new servant of Jacob–he got busy and tried to scrape up–**some kind**–just **any kind**...of blessing for himself...but Issac said 'son...**don't bother...there is nothing left**...

You are bereft–but when you have **dominion...in my opinion**...you will be able to break his yoke–off your **neck!**'

In the meantime–Jacob had to **get away quick–and in a hurry**...'you must run a long ways **from home...son**',–said his mother...because Esau was gonna do some bloodletting...and it didn't matter that he was his brother...!!

We see thru history...**that brothers have been against brothers**–and even to this day–we **haven't advanced much further–in fully accepting each other.**

Although...**we claim to be striving for unity–but the stomping sound and the drum beat–of disunity...tends to drown the harmony of love and peace–as it accelerates–into deteriorations**...of the communities.

Black brothers–are **symbolic to the fables "Cinderella"**...working from sun-to to sun-down–helping to build and birth every **facet of America**–sacrificing their backs and minds for its heritage...but **being denied a fair share of–inheritance.**/ However, there are **a few tokens of** credibility for **accomplishments–yet...What's up with those** that are hidden and exploited–under the skirts of the cruel and grueling stepmother??–of course–there have been some amends–though, most have been pinned on the behinds of their **chil-dren–while their black brothers' achievements are being buried in bereavement–which is lost in the ashes of forgetfulness–there in the cinders–of time! But God is pointing his finger**–these injustices–He will...review!!

And just dues–he will reward! **Yea! Every dime!**

Once...there were two brothers–Aaron and Moses...None other– have been closer. Moses was the **spiritual brain**–Aaron had the **anointed tongue–and both–God had to train**...to interact as one. Later on–Aaron and Miriam–their sister...became **disgruntled resisters... meddling with Moses' wife–and his life.** So-o-o! God, temporarily, turned Miriam white as snow–making her the white "Thang"...opposite of black "Thang" that she had "**raked over the coals**"! Howbeit, their main issues were...**other than**–the **color or the race**...[the same as it is today]. But for them...it was **jealousy of God talking to Moses...face to face!**

We've also read where Joseph's brothers threw him in **a pit**–not knowing that one day–before him they would bow and **sit**...with their fate in his hand–far away in another land. However, two of them had begged for his life–causing the others to sell him–to the–Ishmael-ites– there is the darkness of the night. Hence opening the way for Joseph's dreams-- to magnify.

Finally, the fulfillment of the **Prophesy** came...but Joseph **held no malice–as** he held up his–**gavel**. He ordered their bags to be filled with grain–even to over heaping–while his heart was joyfully leaping–he knew that he was indeed–**His Brothers' Keeper**'!!

We must remember...**that the linking of minds into a positive flow– produces wealth and knowledge–never known before Real power is in the unification of all color–Creed–and races...only the evilness of hatred and hostility–separates! Ignorance and division is civilization in retrogression–and love is the generator–that disintegrates the energies–of enmity and social denigration!!**

Why deny the fact that **we are extensions** of one another–while **working as a unit–called a community? Why are we quick to promul-gate' our differences and separation?**

We like proclaiming that we are pure black–pure white–pure red– pure bred...and ad infinitum! Tweely de dum! Strangely enough–it's never heard about Jesus' love–that purified all races–in the sanctity–of his blood!

There is one single thread which intertwines–in the brotherhood thru generations–in every given situation–Satan uses to bind since eons of times. The **Demonic spirit of–jealousy** is his name...**creating rebellious-ness is his game.** This can be understood–in the study of the hoods. **The decision of being a division–is not about color–but the other...which is the drive for power...administrated by human towers.**

We must stop feeding into this "Thang" and take the blinders off... and make a **change**–in **our families**–in races...and our country...and be an aggressive unit–in executing unity–in our communities! **Lets go forth together**–singing and dancing–breaking our fedders–with **gladness**– putting down Satan's **madness** of racial **discrimination**–and rise up to take our **rightful position on the throne–of equalization**–Wielding our scepter with–dignity and aplomb!! We'll stretch out hands–joining each other with loving hearts–touching our sisters and brothers in harmony and peace–forming a circle of–completeness and **wholeness.** Then we can bring our plates **filled** with **encouragement–immunity** and **opportunity** as we step out in–**boldness**–with **caring** and **sharing** as our–**just dessert...and–when–sisterly–and brotherly love...become a commitment to unity**– The healing process will, then, **begin**–in all of our **communities!**

FOREWOOD
BIG FOOT

While doing research on some of the great black ancestors...I was amazed at their grandeur, while facing undue hardship. Some were right in the throes of slavery...consequently... thousands were murdered. Nonetheless...there would be those that kept rising to succeed–in the face of all kinds of obstacles and atrocities of astronomical odds. The proverb 'only the fittest survive' must have been born out of this era.

During my reviews; I had an upsurge of racial pride...and was impressed with a common thread, first and foremost, our ancestors had strong faith in God. As far as I could determine, the value placed on education rated second to God. They acquired it anyways possible. Sometimes, at their own peril, because this was one of the tools that could be used to crawl out of the muck and mire.

Another impressive note was...when one reached the cotton stalk or tree top...[now it's called the glass ceiling]. He or she reached back to help others with schools...businesses–etc.

I was moved–when I read about the ownership, even then, of all kinds of businesses, which was another point of pride. Unity in community endeavors promoted respect...even to menial industry of big bar'b que sales–'Sadi-dy night' fishfrys–moonshine liquor–home-made brew–and so on. They knew how to make a dollar! But on the other hand, who can lay blame? Something was needed to keep dignity and deaden the pain!

I was inspired knowing–that going to school, then–took a lot of courage–sacrifice and personal dedication–which deserves admiration!

Many were self-taught! I rather think God–taught!! Indeed, these were dark days for 'Blacks' to be educated–amidst other intolerable things–being suffered. But they didn't bow down to–then–legitimate excuses!! Their survival skills were sharpened every wakening moment... even when asleep! Because they knew that > The Big Foot Walked...

BIG FOOT

The Big Foot...Who walks to and fro...
Kicking down doors...to stomp on the poor. Minorities
suffering more–scuffling–shuffling and scrubbing the
floors–so, on it goes.

The foot squishes and squashes...as strong wills are
crushed with moanings and groanings from the mental
anguish...The innermost being is smashed into an
emotional mush of weariness...slashing a naked soul and
heavy spirit–till all hope is gone!

Circumspectly, the little mounds of mush...rise up and
Suddenly, has grown–mentally alert and spiritually
Strong–being guided by God–his staff and rod...by his
Mercy...the tender shoot has been shown...how to seep thru
The thorns and ooze between the toes–to circumvent Big
Foots vicious–Blows...Thereby...rising up from the ashes of
Mashing...and like the Phoenix–meta –morpho-sing
Into brilliant minds and dynamic souls...

The burley booga bear...with the big squashing foot...**was and is**...totally
Unaware that God was...and is...for evermore–in control...His power is
supreme in the superlative degree...and continues throughout history...
and yet to be...Unfold.

Howbeit...we must note...our Father-God was breaking slavery chain
gangs...and alleviating social pains...long before our existence in the era
of slavery...
Nevertheless–no race, more humbly, performed and
endured–with such hardihood. Evenso...God had to
send his angelic swat teams...many times...to draw the lines...
rescuing the abused and executing...the abusers...

Why–he had honored four hundred years of petitions...by
The children of Isra-el...bringing their prayers into
fruition...and plucked them from...a perilous hell.
He called his servant and commanded him–to take a
stand...[translation-] 'Moses quit your fretting...I've
made my selection–and you are chosen to break ole'
Pharoah's iron foot–off my children's over-stretched
neck. I am sending you and Aaron–for my people to
fetch–**and tell Pharoah...I am**–sent you...[Paraphrasing]
'Enough, already!! He's through!!

And then, there was David...A mighty warrior–full of
fear...while Saul–his enemy...hunted him down...with
men and blood-hounds...because he wanted him bad–he
wasn't sharing his throne–with this lad!! Stomping his
Big Foot–he looked...and every branch–he shook...
he was going to squash David–until nothing stood–not
even a sprig of his hair–would be spared.
Saul's chase brought him close...unawares–right under
David's nose...but being tired...he had to sleep awhile–and as he
Snored–David creeped–to cut off a piece of his robe...and quickly
Retreated...When the distance was ample–quite afar–he shouted
to Saul with glee–Ah Ha -!
Look!!...shaking the scrap–he stole–your life could've

also...been on this pole!!!
And then...it was like Tic Tac Toe–to and Fro–In the
wilderness...what a contest! Til God [I imagine] got tired of
the mess...brought Saul home...and gave David his
throne...then they all got some...rest!

The mechanism and method...of the Big Foot never
Stops–never–sleeps–as it creeps...looking for any means
to crush the spirit, emotion and mind...which are made
weary...nevertheless,–sublime. By the tempering of
pressure...it is hard to recognize–that the foot is hiding
under a clever disguise–of love–peace–which covers
deceit...while its ultimate goal is...to demoralize...

The implementation of the "Lynch Law" has not proven in it's
entirety–the theory of per-pe-tu-ity of plantation
mentality.
Only in those cases...in certain places...where this indelible
Demonic footprint...left its mark in the heart–but not in
the head...Howbeit–there is no evidence of mental and
emotional retrogression...
Because God was always on time in–his redressing.

Which brings to mind–when Harriet Tubman was
Stubborn–and the attacker, Big Foot...caused her head to
give her trouble–which left her prostate–almost dead.
However, she refused to be reduced to mental bondage...
and physical carnage. Moreover, she used her handicap
and anointing to map an underground railroad–right in
the lap–and under the adversary's nose...moving
hundreds of slaves–to freedom and safety–through the
crevices–of big foot's toes...

Hey!...Wait!...too late!...The 'Coons' just got away!
Suddenly, another black shoot–sprung up from Big Foot's
mush. Benjamin Banneker...a genius...an astronomer–
mathematician and inventor–who made mockery of the hypothesis–of
the black brain density.
He memorized and reproduced the blueprint of the city
Washington, D.C.–Not one square inch on his rule was–
misconstrued...D.C. was built–on schedule. Even so–he
wasn't through!!...He built the first American Wooden
Clock–and for forty years it didn't stop...
And his almanacs were so precise and reliable...that they
became a household staple, with the Bible...This work of
genius–caused Thomas Jefferson to refute the white
lie–of black inferiority.

The Big Foot raised up with a stronger aim...to stamp out
this growing fungus–of acclaim–not realizing that the
union is necessary --for the power of its brain.
Oh! My! ...Big Foot is posturing again!! Gaining momentum
Ready to slam-dunk the slush beneath the surface–of the
earth.

Oomph...barely, missed **Sarah Breedlove**–as she surged
towards the light above–better known as **C.J.
Walker**–a seven year old orphan.
spent years–enduring tension and stress...
As she labored as a–laundress...Well, the steam...kept
her hair in little knotted–kinks...which caused her to
think...must be some way to control this mess–so...
her own hairdress–she did concoct–her friends bought the
product and invested in her stock–making her an
immediate success...and the first black–millionairess!

Oops! Missed again! Big Foot sloshed and stomped–until
He pushed up–**Miff-lin Wis-ter Gibbs**–who had a
childhood of very little joy–supporting his mother as a
twelve year old-boy–But determination and
perseverance– brought him into his destiny–as America's
first black municipal judge–being in a good
position–there–as an advocate of black affairs
because God had heard all of his prayers.

Clump! Clump!...'son of a slave...I'm kicking him back in the
baboon cave...he must learn how to behave...where did he
go??? Why! There!!–in his pharmacy store with a formal
medical degree–the first Black American to obtain–them
both!! The scoop was too broad of a scope–for Big Foot to
see or read...so, he couldn't impede the approach...of **Dr.
James McCune Smith**...Oh well! Just another
contradiction–of the offensive racial–Myth!!
Oh! Oh! A strange voice–Big Foot is annoyed...and again
on a rampage–trying to be slick...sneaking up like a
fox–but got tricked and stuck in his own plot...His
stomping motion–suddenly stopped...because

Matthew Alexander Henson–had jumped out of the slush
pot!!
Plodding along to the North Pole–he and Robert Peary...
snow blinded and weary...both brave and bold–as they
plodded thru the arctic cold–barely able to walk...
Only the two of them...left–to talk.
But determined...Henson forged ahead...as he prayed and
paved their way. At last...while stopping at the right spot–Robert
Peary caught up–somewhat late...with his surveyor's tape -
to confirm that they had made it to the top...

Overjoyed–Matt opened his frozen bag–and pulled out the
American Flag...and in the bitter Arctic cold–he, proudly,
Pushed it in a hole...there...at the North Pole.

As we can see Big Foot is always hanging a rope on a tree...
or trying to kick up with tenacity–the eternal
root. It roams like a mad dog in heat–trying to stomp
Out the poor and making the strong–weak.

In spite of the efforts–of the iron foot to destroy the
power of the roots...of the black race [and others] thru
struggles and strifes–continue to thrive and
survive. The list is long that has come up through–rank
and file.

Booker T. Washington...and **George Washington
Carver**...both a credit to their race and country...no one
can deny...
Crispus Attucks...For American Independence...was the first
to die...

Barbara Jordan...first black elected to the Texas
Senate...spearheaded laws no bring equality to all...as a
United States Representative...
Maggie Lena Washington...The first woman bank
president–in American's History...described as having a
business acumen of–brilliancy.
Mary McLeod Bethune–founded her first school on $1.50 -
who was not discouraged...and for her recompense of
being steadfast–Bethune Cookman College emerged...

These...and thousands of other outstanding people -
Refused Big Foot's smashing reminders–to 'stay in their

place'!!...which is a phraseology of death and doom–Where
A Future of Darkness Looms!!!

Glory Hallelujah!!...The Holy Spirit was there with his
Embrace–to lead them–under His wings of–Godly
Grace!!–As they **seeped** thru ole' Big Foot's toes and under
the arch that moored...**around** his corns...bunions and
crusty heels–even **between** the skin...that peeled. Then
swiftly–like an arrow's–penetration–revealed the
nucleus–of ethnic indoctrination–a mental infiltration...
practiced for generation...
This systematic technique must be, consistently–resisted!

However, those that receive revelation...seize the
opportunity–to make great cultural strides–after
discovering Big Foot's...lies!! And continue to march with
dignity–displaying American black–pride. The
productivity of multi-facet talents–are significant
contributions–to their country–and to their race...so
why the derision Why the Exclusion?
Ha!!–me thinketh–delusion of grandeur!!!

Pages and pages and sheets and sheets–of names of blacks
that were–'the first'–in their various fields of
endeavors–for centuries–are still incomplete.
So–research and studies should be a prerequisite–for
home training–since black culture–progress and
knowledge is limited and also nil...in the public school
system...By having no role model–or positive image...this opens
the doors of young and tender minds–to receive deni-gration
and idiotic remarks–like 'monkey and coon brains'–as
valid assessments of their intelligence.–Nevertheless black
contributions of the past are rich and endless,–but not taught

and is treated with condescension and pretension .. of being non-existent!!!

Whump! **Whomp**!–of the Big Foot–springing up from the whooshing–another reed from the root. A passion for racial freedom–he stood.
The change of social structure was focused on God's purpose–for the world. **Martin Luther King, Jr.** was an inspiration to all who saw and heard. His words–'Let **Freedom Ring**.'–still lives on the unfurls–with resonance... Not only for his race...but for all downtrodden people -- who has no shining light–in their darkest night.

Evenso!! He had a dream–a living beam of hope–that he shared–with heavy hearts and souls–
That were bared. He broadened the scope–further... To include and declare...that the human race–who's in despair–in compiled of sisters and brothers–
Who are, all, under–our Father's care!

The Big Foot keeps raising up–aiming for the minds and the bodies–that keeps growing and flowing–right thru his toes. Oh!–Bow-Wow! They are not spooky!!...these are... an incredible people of integrity and intelligence– misrepre-sented–as coons and baboons. Now we have to do a correction in Webster's Dictionary–and real soon!! We must not be caught up–in the proverbial, 'Dog chasing his tail' -- syndrome...which is the norm–Purposely, placed in mind–so that you miss the game trail's sign. It's not about the name calling of nigger...nigros...niggur... or–nigga'–which is a stigma of bondage–purposely–to ignite emotional flames–of rage.

Nor get caught up in the political correctness of being
called–'Black!;
But rather–once we have scaled the invidious wall...how
can we give something back–is the question–for all!!!

When the discovery is made–to look up–not down...from
chasing the tail–around and around...then the light becomes
brighter–that it's not in the might–but in the
matter...Because God up there–has given power to the
reproduction genes–down here! Hence–The DNA is
enslaved!

Let's be apprised of some real facts–stop the hang-ups
about colors of being...yellow meal–yams–cauliflower–
butterscotch–or black!
And study the reasons–ways–whys and hows–to make a
change...so that a people...can stop suffering from–lack.
And use the energy of the brains...to decipher the black fallacy.
The 'Divide and Conquer' theory–is to gain the power of
the phallus and this–Big Foot for eons has concealed...
Containing it in the crevices–creases and the callous–of his heel.

Now, you see...since Big Foot is exposed–no need to shudder
behind your emotional door–meet him headlong–which
approach the **'reproach'** with generations of rich stories–which
contradicts and discloses–the big slavidic lie.
Loose Willie Lynch's mental and emotional Nigga Tic And
Don't Blank an Eye–nor look back...then ask how to spell
and say...Nah-Nah!!–Not African American! That's mixed
and mashed, also–I've heard–'Affa American–'Affrin'
American–'Aff American...but what's the other word??
Can you spell and say it?--- **B-l-a-c-k...You got it...Black!**
Dr. King was right! Anybody can say that!!!

But be aware! That Big Foot walks on both sides of the
fence–is now stamping families into shambles–which isn't
restricted to racial boundaries–leaving homes and lives
floundering...hearts torn–without defense!!

He kicked and stomped–until he put God out of the schools --
no more to be guided by the 'Golden Rule'...So that he could
substitute–drugs, violence, hate and prostitutes–which are
acceptable to the pre-conditioned off springs–even to the
unpleasantness it brings. Parents of all colors–suffer the same
fate!...Now–the stomping and beatings **they have to take...**
that comes from Big Foot's kids...[**not 'Ba-Ba's**]

Howbeit...out of sufferings–comes spiritual light...There is
no sense to the fight–Jesus died for the whole human race
and in all nations–are his creations.

His blood was shed–because he loved us and when He rose
from the bottom of Hell–grace and mercy were like
tinkling sounds–of liberty bells...and on his wings --
they were ringing–as He soared–swifter than the fastest
eagle. His ascension–was like a blinking of the eyes --
Blending with the stars–and the cloudy skies. His
graceful move upward–was priestly and regal, while
rising–gliding with benevolence–toward the
Heavens–where he sits besides Father-God and before man's
Ancestors–as the personal priest–and spiritual intercessor
of all races. Jesus Christ...our Savior of redeeming grace who loved
us enough to shed his blood.

PREFACE TO THE HOLY SPIRIT

This particular writing is very dear to me, and it's one of the most inspirational pieces that I have ever written; because of the very nature of my spiritual and emotional encounter with the higher power, I hear you say, --- "**Hunh**??" ... what she talking about, now? **Well**–I am **speaking** of–a glorious interaction with the Holy Spirit!

I will start at the beginning; when I was introduced to Him, on April 28, 1997; almost five years ago:

Joyce Seabrook encouraged me to go to the intercessory prayer meeting. There were several women, Joyce and I were the only **Blacks**... [simply noted, for the purpose of a better vantage point]. 'What's Intercessory Prayer?" It is, basically, a group of people praying in agreement for different issues and causes, involving families–friends–Churches–the world–each other...and of course whatever else comes up in the free flowing discussions. We had taken time from our jobs and other busy schedules, to spend this time to cry out to the Lord. Faye Dean, a woman full of faith and...'on fire for God," with an apparent anointing of the Holy Spirit, was the leader of the group. She opened the meeting with scripture reading and prayer. Subsequently, I was introduced and the session began.

I will try to set the scene for you. There was no whooping and hollering...jumping up and down...nor nasal secretions and mouth slob-bering–happenings. The atmosphere was calm with quiet emotions; nevertheless, feelings could be felt, as discussions became lively.

I don't know, today, [even my journal didn't help me] how the conversation got around to me with the question; "Henrietta have you received

111

the baptismal of the Holy Spirit?" I remember feeling, somewhat, outside of this spiritual arena; and seemingly, I thought about how much God had been in my life, so, I was not a stranger to his divine guidance! "Didn't he bring me here, over 2,600 miles away from home, children, family, and friends...not knowing any- body...and isn't He providing friends...extended family...and assistance for me and John-Mark, since being here?" [Of course, I can go back even further than this experience, which is another 'Book'] But, I have been under the shadow of God's hand all of my life...because my grandmother, Lenora Lampkins had sown the spiritual seed in us, and very well!

"Um-mn...have I received the Holy Spirit? Didn't he give me confirmation, when he had John-Mark to read the scripture from Deuteronomy 31:6 to encourage me because he was directing this move? [This boy didn't know how to call out scriptures...let alone enunciate Deuteronomy. He read "Be of good courage, fear not, not be afraid of them: for the Lord thy God, he it is that doth go with thee. He will not fail thee nor forsake thee."...Well, I took this as a personal sign because I had been experiencing a bit of fear, about moving into a different culture. I said, "Boy, only the Holy Spirit could have given you that!" Then I, mentally, went back to the question, "Have I received the Holy Spirit?" Well, didn't he put all of these beautiful people in my path... my neighbors, who look after us and friends that feel like family?" I remembered Pastor Neal's prophecy when Joyce, Barbara and I went to the alter for prayer...'The Spirit is saying something about sisters...that's all I am getting.' But I was thinking about my biological sisters and did not associate these prophetic words, until later. [I think, they thought the same].

"Have I received the **Baptismal** of the Holy Spirit?" This must be different. I looked at her and rounded the 'O' and said, "No-o." She pressed, "Well...do you want to receive it?" Slowly, I said, "Yes-s." But I was thinking, "At some other time, I need some time to analyze this." Oft-times, we have a fear of the unknown...now, I know that mine was from **weak faith**–which I thought was strong!

Speaking in tongues, [or other tongues] was stressed, rather than the Baptismal of the Holy Spirit. Also, that you have to pray for it to happen. Matter-of-fact, 'Miss Marsha', a strong believer and close friend, promoted and encouraged this spiritual aspect...and we did pray...but, apparently, it was not the time nor the place...besides I refused to flap my tongue! Meantime, Fay's eyes were piercing right through my thoughts, saying, "if so, we can pray right now!" and I thought, "Right now!" But I, bravely, said, "Yes, I do." Don't get me wrong, I

Really wanted the experience, though deep-rooted in my mind–was doubt. I just wanted it to be true and genuine.

So, the Leadlady [Faye] and all of the others, stood praising and thanking the Lord with hands raised. It seemed that this went on for hours [it really wasn't!] I just have no idea how long, we were in this stance. However, my arms became very tired and as they began to slump, I realized that someone was helping me to keep them up [Joyce was one of them]...and I kept praising and thanking the Lord.

Pausing here, for this scene to be envisioned; I was encircled by the other sisters, along with Faye, who stood in front of me and most of them were speaking in other tongues, including Faye. Joyce was standing on one side of me, to help hold my arm and another was on the other side, assisting the other arm. [A thought is running thru my mind as I write this–that we pray the Holy Spirit in and we pray the "Devil **out!**"] Faye was going strong as she would say, "The Holy Spirit is right here, wanting to come in!" and I thought, "I can't hold my arms up any longer!...Even with all of this help!" I felt drained!

At this point, I was thinking, "Can I speak in tongues [I thought 'tongues', because I had been programmed in the past that this is what this was all about]...I'll have to try another time. Meanwhile, they were all going strong, as they spoke in other tongues. It is noteworthy to admit, that I had no concept of what was suppose to happen, except being able to speak in other tongues. Well, feeling that it wasn't gonna happen; I began to relax, or you may say; I had given up.

Then suddenly!!! Everything started happening, at once...it was like an explosion!!...stretching and expanding from the lower part of my stomach, all the way up to the top or thru my head; it gave me an intense headache...it felt as if it was coming off; I remember wishing for the pain to stop. Simultaneously, the tears burst forth like water was dashed on my face and along with this episode–groanings and moanings–similar to a hard belly laugh. It seemed that the sound was coming from a depth, in a valley, even from someone else, that was inside of me. Faye was saying "That's Him...that's the Holy Spirit wanting to speak... let Him speak!" I recall the sound, "Hough!! Hough!!...more guttural groaning in a continuous, "Hough-Hough!" uttered all the while, I was being expanded and stretched.

I felt a Herculean strength. Samson must have been cognizant of such strength, only in hundreds of multiples, when he pulled massive pillars, of a great building, together, with all of his might, until it collapsed; killing three thousand people. [Of course, it killed him, too!] I am aware that the comparison of strength is unequal to his level...with the exception that both types of strengths–were supernatural.

Also, worth mentioning, is that the Sisters were being 'slain in the spirit' around me. Notwithstanding, the news got around at Church. The Pastor and everyone was excited about the "Good News!" I was congratulated, as if I had just gotten married...and in retrospect...**That's exactly what happened**!! How I praise and thank Him for just this bit of revelation of knowing that–'He's for real!!!'

I am finding that the Holy Spirit takes me in steps...on levels, [if you will]. Perhaps he does it for all...I am not an authority. I am discovering that there is, too much for any one person to ever experience, or know about Him.

In sharing this beginning knowledge of the presence of the Holy Spirit, will help, somewhat, my readers to understand my desire to know more. Much later, when I came to Grace and Restoration; my Pastors, began teaching on the Holy Spirit and the evidence of speaking in [other] tongues. I made it known of my seeking this evidence, because after the Holy Spirit's Baptism...there was not another sound from me.

Yet...speaking in [other] tongues is a common practice among many. We had several discussions and teachings on this subject.

One Sunday, we had a visiting Pastor, who did a beautiful teaching on the Holy Spirit–and at the end of this message; an invitation was extended to **those** seeking the Baptismal of the Holy Spirit, to come up and receive the laying on of hands. Well, it seemed that all eyes were upon **me**!...and rightly so, I was the only one there, not speaking in [other] tongues!! This incidence was similar to April 1997, when Faye and all of the other eyes were piercing me!...and now it was happening in April 2001! Well, back to the point; so, they kept looking at me and talking about what the "Word" said on this matter. Finally, with no way out...[because I couldn't pretend any longer that: "They weren't talking to me. I spoke up and said, I have no doubt that I have been baptized by the Holy Spirit"...but, I added, "I haven't spoken in [other] tongues." Consequently, I was not led [by the Holy Spirit] to go up for the 'laying on of hands'. However, I just wanted him to do it without anybody's help...my feelings were, He didn't need it! I wanted it to be a supernatural experience, as before. Basically, I am not an emotional person, and for the most part–low-keyed...but since my spiritual experiences and epic poetry writings...seemingly, I am doing an about-face!

One day, after continuing to think about this; I started to talk to the Father, Jesus and the Holy Spirit. I told them how I felt about this matter and how I believed in them and their power. So, why should anyone have to lay hands...since He made my tongue? Doesn't he give it the power to speak?...in whatever language? Isn't it His power source that controls my whole body! Also, why should the glory go to someone else? Besides...how would I really know that the Holy Spirit spoke through me? I told Father God, Jesus and the Holy Spirit that I submit my body and my tongue to them; willingly, and was ready for the Holy Spirit to speak...because **It belonged to them**!

On April 12, 2001, approximately 12 o'clock noon, I was sitting at my kitchen table in a contemplative prayer about this most important concern when...**suddenly a quickening** in the midst of my words of

English, **my tongue felt like something grabbed it and zoomed!** [imagine fishing and your pole give a jerk and the cork sinks quickly in the water!] I could hear the words of strange sounds...had no idea, what I was saying! But the Holy Ghost took me on a spiritual ride that I will never forget, as long as I live! I was conscious of riding giant ocean waves, while I envisioned a giant Dolphin, but I was as one with it and the water was gently rolling...thrusting us above and through the waves...and I felt light and was laughing and speaking this unknown language. No! I don't really care who believes this...all I know is that it happened!...and I thank Father God for not letting me leave this world before experiencing this heavenly joy!! **NOW...I KNOW WITHOUT A DOUBT THAT THE HOLY SPIRIT IS SUPERNATURAL AND REAL**!! Daily I thank and welcome the Holy Spirit's presence...I praise my Holy Spirit's presence...**I praise my Holy Family with all that they give me to praise them with**!!

Howbeit, I was trying to express this beautiful experience to my Pastors and other members...which was not easy to do, because it seemed like a fantasy. This very essence of Spiritual beauty could not be put into words. Nevertheless, one of my sisters, Alma said, "Write a poem about it. Sister Davison." I opened my mouth to say, "Nah, I can't"...but then I thought, "What a challenge!" I think I'll try rising to the occasion. Hence...the poem "HOLY GHOST" it is incorporated in this Book!

THE HOLY GHOST

God was parturient with the creation of man...animals...fowls of the air...seas filled with various mammals...that were rare...a hoard of creeping things under and upon the earth...a world to hang in the universe. His creatures were to live...love...play... mate...and on Him depend as His friends. He, even, gave them the choice to choose their fate–and with freewill–give Him joy–but not as an animated toy...So, He endowed them with five senses...and by His Spirit–He instilled in the midst of this origination–God was thrilled!!

He called for the **"Word"** then the **universe began to rumble...like thunder...exhibiting strong vibrations**...it was **time** for the **delivery of the creation**...and as he spoke...**the "Word" prepared** for the **manifestation**...He began to **mold** and **shape** each–**creature**...being directed by the Father...as to their **characteristic–feature.** Then God said, 'This is good!' --- Now...we must hurry!!! Man is coming upon the scene. The "Word" got busy–making a **flashing dash**–moving **faster** than the **speed of light**...He began to construct him–**sculpting the dirt**–in the image of them. Envision God saying, My theme in this specific scheme...will include our **D.N.A.**–in their **spiritual genes**...the "Word" then **scooped** a big lump of love...**thumping it** into man's heart...with **a thud**–both **beamed...knowing that they made an excellent team!!!**

When the universe and all the creatures in the world were suspended–supposedly God said...'Now it's time for all to be set in motion'... He **then called out to the Holy Spirit from the four winds–and from the waters and waves of every ocean–and as He came–His breath was a vapor of pulsating radiation** and while Father and Son watched...

the Holy Ghost encompassed the whole creation–with His Divine breathing–of fiery penetration–covering all organism–from the tiniest microbe–to the highest in the heavens...moon...stars and the sun... using **His breath as a majestic robe. Then, suddenly, the whole universe began to rock**...ticking and tocking like a...Grandfather's clock. Under His hand of ad-minis-trant power...the job was well done...and all became living beings...that very..."in the beginning" hour...because "**to be**"...God, simply, commanded and allowed us.

Finally...after this sequel...the man and woman were living well– then up jumped the devil–to make their life a living hell. He being full of evil–watched their fun and frolic with envy...while they enjoyed the camaraderie with Father God...**of whom Satan had intense enmity**.

So he decided to invade the dark sides of their heart and waited for the right moment–to present his plan of deceit. Sly--ly, telling them the big 'snake lie'–convincing them that the fruit–they could eat and would not die–but make them like gods–with eyes opened to good and evil. At that–he, probably, smiled...[**the sleazy weasel**] **thinking...yeah**!!!–your eyes will be open and–wide...when you behold your naked sinful selves... over yonder–you will hide...**behind the leaves–of the big 'stanky' ramp trees**. And, since, God's command were not harkened–they were kicked out of the garden–with their days–forever darkened.

Satan was an enemy to God and the first family...and his evil doings still con-tin-ues...thru the centuries his hostility perpetuates...and aggression escalates because of his jealous–iss-ues. He, still, viciously attacks families. Unprepared parents are confused as they clamber to find the answer–investigating in all of the wrong places–while the children [Rek-re-ate] recreate–on the demonic **stage**. Naturally...we love them passionately...and when we listen to their lies or denials...we rationalize and sympathize–letting our anger fade away into compassion... **oops**!–**watch out**!! We have just been **kicked to the curb...and under their–incorrigible feet**!! Their audacious behavior is excused–with the age old **adage**–"**The devil made them do it**"...**while parents quickly**

concede to the deceit. Inevitably–the lateness of wisdom come to bear... when their little hands–go up in the air–giving a hi-five sign–with a loud..."Yes"!!–as parenthood bows in disgrace–and acquiesce!

Eventho...Satan encourages corrupt behavior .. it does not matter that he plants the wicked seeds...unscrupulous actions are evil deeds... thereby, debts...are due and payable...**God has decreed**!!! Therefore, when the children...Adam and Eve...opened the doors to the beginning of sin–the heavenly peace was then disturbed --- upon all the earth. Let's imagine God–our Father, who is so merciful; say...'**un-unh-unh!!! My poor babies!!! They will need a savior–Jesus, my son**, will you help them out? They are down there being foolish and floundering about... and he said 'I will, Father'...so God chose and prepared the body of the Virgin Mary...because He had to come thru a Holy Channel–first he moved to squash all potential scandal–by sending his Holy Angel to apprise–so Mary wouldn't be surprised...for by the **Holy Ghost... she would conceive–bringing forth a son**–and for man's sins–he was destined to–**intercede**.

As Jesus prepared for His ministry–with optimism–He went into the river of Jordan–for His baptism. While **coming straightway out of the water–praying looking up–He saw–the Holy Spirit from above– gliding with wings–in the winds–descending upon him in the form of a dove– consecrating Him with the baptism of fire– preparing Him for the days of trial**. And as Jesus was caressed–with his love–the words were spoken–while the heaves were opened...saying, '**This is my beloved son...of whom, I am well pleased!**" And Jesus, joyously, received... knowing that the Holy Ghost power–he would **surely need**–to carry him thru–**his final hour**.

Subsequently...Jesus died upon the cross and on the evening of His resurrection–He blowed upon His disciples the breath of the Holy Spirit–personally, the **comforter** he was presenting–who the Father was sending to help them in their ministry. Saying–"When He hears from us–your hearts will be searched–being your counselor–full of knowledge...He will teach and instruct you–in all things...even how to use the principles of logic.

Howbeit...the created man was done–**indeed**–but his spiritual metamor-phosis–would then begin–when the Holy Spirit was–purposed to come.

Jesus said, [paraphrasing]. He will abide with you forever–giving you facts...so that your messages will have a powerful impact...**"But now, I must go to my Father and at this time**...you cannot follow" [paraphrasing] The Holy Ghost will guide and interpret–bringing to remembrance **all that I've taught...and thru you–miracles will be–wrought.**

While Jesus admonished...they were astonished and watched His departure with heaviness in their hearts–holding on to every word. They didn't dare stir–staring–**eyes brimming over with tears as Jesus slowly ascends–and finally disappears.**

Subsequently...men, women and children tarried–with Jesus' last words in their minds and hearts–they carried. Waiting on the coming of the Holy Ghost–were a hundred and twenty–at the most.

Praises and prayers were set up–while hovering there in the upper room...then!! Suddenly!! Hearing a rustling noise–like a mighty rushing of winds–with the intensity of roaring flames–swooping them up in His Spirit–as He consumed each one–while they pressed together in great fear. His mighty presence–visibly–overwhelmed all therein–as He appeared–yet...they received Him–with trembling–and joyous tears.

Assuredly...he came filling up the house–where they were sitting... some on the couch–and others praying in a crouch. He felled upon each one–with cloven tongues liken to fire...as he sat upon all–taking them by surprise–giving them utterance as they cried–speaking in other tongues–at the top of their lungs...while multitudes–miles around heard and moved in as close as they could–to hear the words–thinking that they were drunk or joking–listening with their mouths and ears opened–not a soul stirred–exclaiming that their own language–they understood...each one–his own dialect...and since that day–unto now...

the Holy Spirit's dramatic entry creates the same effect. Evenso...His person will conform to the spirit of the soul–which has invited Him–to enter.

And to every modern day Ezekiel–God is saying [and I paraphrase] go into this generational valley of bones...that are arid...brittle...and dry. I want you to **preach! and prophesy**...even though–you feel helpless and weak–even when your approaches seems–hopeless, and the people are in regression–**prophesy and teach! Prophesy and cry out!!! with a boom-ing voice**...make a loud noise–that will shake and rattle–as you go into battle–so that these dried bones will come together...bone-to-his-own bone...and I will strengthen and make them strong. I will pull the **cover of sinew and skins upon them tight...toughen them like raw hide...for the spiritual flight!!**

Now...you Ezekiels–of the 21ˢᵗ century–**pitch your voices to the winds and prophesy**...giving the Holy Spirit–entry to come in and say "**Thus said the Lord God...come from the four winds...'O' breath and breathe upon these slain–that they may live!**" The Holy Spirit–then–will come with a strong blow of breath...and the dry bones that are standing **upon** their **feet...will become whole and complete–as, an exceedingly, great army!!** And He will continue–to engulf the whole world–in–around and thru it. **And, yes,**...like children–we can, assur-edly, curl up in his bosom–and even snuggle–**the good–the bad–and the ugly**...As He imparts His consuming–fire–to all who request with a sincere desire–and of course–the choice is freely made the case–by an individual faith.

Oh! Holy Ghost...Let us feel your presence...over and around us... as you glow. We welcome you–the **Supernatural Force–of River of Waters–to be our comforter**–and our guide in all the spaces that we breathe–we ask you to–forever abide. Live within us and by our sides–with your holy power–applied.

Your **breath surges** thru our **bodies...causing us to soar to new spiri-tual heights**–when your **spirit swells within us from the expressions** of your holy essence–like the rustlings of the winds–and the rising of the waves...equal to the roaring of the ocean...yet...gentle–as a summer breeze...that waltz tenderly with the tree of...multicolor leaves !!!

Notwithstanding...the intensity of your power is **nigh to bursting**–and the body cannot bear up to the **strength of the thrusting**–except in the realm of your spirit–as you come forth **like lightning bolts–carrying us on waves of ecstasy** [ecstas-c]–while the **billowing rippling water overflows...yet**–calm as a peaceful sea.

The frequency of your voice...comes in hi-low–**pitches**–like the sounds of the **waves–switching**...moving back and forth–**like giant wings who are bringing**–the utterance of **groanings and moanings**–in a melodious tongue–of **singing**.

Perhaps bubbling **laughter of gaiety**...or the sounds of a **swirling–babbling–brook**–swiftly moving–while fading.

Oh! Let us linger with you–Holy Ghost–and you with us–in this **rapturous** and **reverent peace**–tarry here with us–a bit longer. You are welcome here–**indeed! Let us be immersed in you**–as we are carried to **an unknown** spiritual level–with **joyous tears streaming**...while letting us see just a glimpse...**of the Heavenly Heaven!**

A-AH-H–being on this journey with you...no other experience can be liken–or compared–as I am **caught up and captured–with such intense rapture**...

O-OH-H–**Holy Spirit**–your entity is **exalting–glorious and magnificent**. You are the great and **mighty power**–of our father and savior–and thru this very **quin-tes-sence**–their **omnipotence**–is personified–which is expressed by your–**Holy presence!!!**

A MEMORIAL TO A SPECIAL NIECE...
LOUISE LOCKETT

Louise; Your pilgrimage here on earth...
Was like a spirited dove...
Constantly in flight–full of life and love...
Perhaps...incongruent to me–but yourself...
You had to be.
Nevertheless...You must have commune...
With Father God and our Savior...
Who looked beyond your behavior–I assume
And discovered–when He peered into your heart...
That you were His...right from the start///
On July 18th, 2001...unto January 20th, 2002
An additional six-months of time–God extended to you
A double-triple blessing–He gave...
When on July the 18th–you accepted Jesus...
And–I–Am–Sure!...that on that day...
You were, also, saved!
One day, I was praying...for your healing...
Sitting at my kitchen table–with a sad feeling...
The Holy Spirit–hearing me...
Said, "Call and pray for/with her"...and I said,
'How can this be?
She is in surge-ry–even if she isn't...
She cannot speak...

And He said, "You have to press!"
So at His request...I began to seek–His assignment...I did complete
And to my amazement...
Your surgery had been–redressed///
Well...Satan got busy to block the message...
That Jesus had his arms opened...
As you had been praying–and hoping...
But–the Holy Ghost...Kicked down the doors...
And the other demonic forces–He floored...
As they tried to hinder–the good news...
That Jesus had heard your emotional cries...
And your presence with Him–would not be denied...
Nor will your soul be...refused...All because–He loves you!!!!

© January 20, 2002

THE COVER STORY

As I came to the closing of these writings and began to prepare for the compilation; A thought came to mind that I had not given the book a title, nor did I have a design in mind for the cover. One day, some of John-Mark's little art work in school came to my attention and I said, "Ah-ha! He like s to try his hand at drawing... just maybe..." Well -l-l...I know that he's no Picasso...Michelangelo...or Carl Burrows; but he does pretty good...and sometimes, is quite creative.

So, I called John-Mark in California and discussed the book; telling him that it needed a special cover. I asked, "Do you think you can draw something special for it? But, listen!...I want you to **think** with your spirit and be guided by it." He said, "I can do that, Moms Dear." "Ok, but don't throw up no, mess...boy!", I said, So, later, I received a drawing of two hands...(both his) with a shooting star from one to the other–depicting our journey from California to Beckley, West Virginia. In the right hand...he drew the facsimile of mountains that we had passed on our way. I thought, "this may work...but only one of these hands... hu-um! And I know just the person that can bring all this together and that is"...yes! you guessed correctly,...**Mr. Carl Bu**rrows!...and he did it again!...a magnificent painting! He not only captured the spirit of the **physical journey**, but the universal spiritual journey of us all!! That's awesome,...don't you think??

I was showing the painting to my friend, Sister Alma, and as we were discussing a place for my picture...which we both agreed on the position where the sun-face was; she came up with the idea of putting John-Mark's picture there. We both laughed at the idea that it may increase sales! Then, I began to give it some **serious** thought! Notwithstanding, he was in a vision that God gave to me, approximately, two years prior to his birth. He was shown as a baby in a hand; a hand to a voice that I addressed as "Lord" when I was asked "Who's going to take this child?" After rearing two children of my own and four grandchildren...what do you think my answer was? You got it! I said, "Not me Lord, because I have done my share of raising children!" WHO is gonna take this child?" (and those of you, who have heard the Hold Spirit's voice–know; he speaks few words, or sometimes–one word...even in a very still voice... however, he can also, be louder than a boom-box).

The voice became stronger, then I really began to plead my case because I was, indeed, getting the message that he was pointing this baby in my direction. So, I said, again, "Not me Lord, my grandchildren are in their late teens and will be on their own real soon, now and then I can get some rest and enjoy some of the things I've put on hold; I was talking real fast to get my point across. Meanwhile the hand with the baby inside was moving semicircle [liken to an offer of hors d'oeuvres at a party.]...**WHO IS GOING TO TAKE THIS CHILD?**" Not only did the voice get louder...but it boomed –more like a big rumble of thunder! [this whole scene was taking place high in the heavens] and simultaneously, as I watch–a giant beam of light went down into the center of my family room..I knew then 'what was up with that!' The Lord was sending him, anyway; over my protest and objections, [I object, your honor!] so, I changed my plea to oral obeisance and said. "Lord, I will take him, but you will have to help me with him." [a thought here...I don't know why I said, "take him", there wasn't a way for me to see the gender!] Of course, I know that he doesn't have to help me with anything that he doesn't want to–but thank God for him being a great and awesome God...because he certainly helps me with this child!! Even though; it's like being on the tail end of a 'pop the whip' game; maybe some of you can remember this game, where several children caught hands and ran like wild fire and the head group would stop quickly to violently, whip all the tail-enders in a snake-like motion, and the ones that were riding the tail would get slung up in the tree tops [well, almost!] before bursting their buttocks on the ground! I didn't ride that tail end! Unh-unh!! And guess what? I could not ride the WHIP of the 'game of life, either',–without The Hold Spirit riding with me, to keep the rump bumping to a bare minimum.

In my next book, I'll share how the Lord directed this child to me... or me to him!

Now...about the picture chosen. As I was looking for a current picture of John-Mark; I came across some of his baby pictures...mulling over them and reflecting on how the time had flown by-since five days old, until now, and how good God has been to both of us. He continues to have him in his hand, [physically and spiritually] today; as he was shown to me in the [spiritual] vision, almost fourteen years ago. He put me therein, too; in the shadow of his hand, alongside of John-Mark!

The grandchildren would dress him up in all kinds of crazy things and take pictures of him...[I think this is why he is such a 'ham' today!] and I saw this specific picture (over a year old) which made me think of an 'old man' in a baby's body who is coming down from the mountains on his transmigration. I thought "This is it! How symbolic of life coming on earth in the spirit!" Hence, the reason for this particular picture in the 'hand on the cover. Thanks to the Holy Spirit, who just gave me the title to this book–"**INFANCY TO INFINITY IN THE SHADOW OF HIS HAND.**"

INFANCY TO INFINITY IN THE SHADOW OF HIS HAND

INTRODUCTION

A
pproximately three years had passed, since my first published book of epic poetry, which was done in September 1999. I must say that the second time around is as difficult to get started as was the first time.

I will begin with Mea culpa and apologies, to people; [important ones] whose names were omitted from Book #1...and who have been, tremendously, encouraging, while helping me on my pilgrimage. Since they were not mentioned in my last book, I will rectify this now; because it was not intentional. God has put each person in my pathway to help me on my way and I pray the help is reciprocal. Sometimes I am given a hand with my son...a smile and prayer of reassurance...or cheerful conversation, while being at my lowest ebb.

Well, I was so chagrined, when one of our unmentioned friends approached me with, "I was one of the first ones that you all met here in Beckley...and you left my name out of your book!"...and I think I muttered, 'I sure thought you were included.' Actually, it was hard for me to believe it, and anyway, how did she know this; she didn't get one of the books? So, I decided to review the 'Introduction' and sure enough...her name was nowhere in the book. Needless to say, I was quite humiliated, especially, when all of the thoughts came rushing back to how we met!

My son, John-Mark and I had just moved here to Beckley, and of course as aforementioned; we didn't know anyone. So one day, we decided to stop at this big store...just exploring, you might say. My son went one way and I another...and suddenly, I heard this lady gushing. "Oh-h that's the nicest complement!" and at first I didn't pay any attention because I wasn't in eyesight, but as she talked I realize she must have been talking to John-Mark, who doesn't meet strangers, and as I moved closer...Yep! It was he! He was busy flattering and she was feasting on every morsel of his complements! As I came in full view, I could see why. Ms. Gloria Smith was a very attractive lady, who was beautifully dressed and my son was impressed...and so was I...because she seemed o nice and friendly! But, of course, John-Mark can draw anyone into conversation. So, we briefly greeted, as I apologized for his forwardness...but she assured me that it was alright.

Anyways, when we left Value City, John-Mark had given her our telephone number and he knew what kind of car she was driving, The same night, to my surprise, she called; and we chatted about us being new in town and hadn't known anyone before we moved here. Subsequently, she invited us over for dinner, and I accepted, based on my feeling that she was trustworthy. But later on, she confessed that her mother, who was recuperating at her home, warned her about bringing strangers into her home. We both had a good laugh about that!

There were visiting relatives, who were also having dinner with us. I met Mrs. Arthelia Smith, Gloria's mother, who I liked instantly. I will never forget, when she said, "Henrietta, you seem like a Christian lady, will you pray for me?" And I said, "I sure will!"...but I thought she was talking about including her in my prayers. She said, "I mean now!"...and I prayed. She has been endeared to me ever-since, and close enough for me to call her 'Arthelia'...and John-Mark to call her "Grandma Smith." He thought that Ms. Gloria belonged to him only, because she spoils him. The Smiths are now members of our extended family.

I first met Ms. Jacqui Bland when we moved here on the twenty-fourth of December 1996. [I had previously met Pastor Earline Neal in November of 1995, in her profession as Property Manager who found the house for us]. She came with Pastor Earline Neal to bring a beautiful small white Christmas tree. They pondered on finding a good spot for it in the living room...[which did not matter, one iota; because there was not a 'stick' of furniture to be seen!!] but finally, they located a place near the window there in the emptiness of the room, and proceeded to decorate it for John-Mark. Pastor Neal said, "Don't worry about Christmas dinner, because I will bring it to you all!" I just gave Jesus praise for looking out for us, and putting these special people in out path. The furniture and dishes had not arrived; so we slept on the floor and ate fast food style...consequently, had accepted our fate of Christmas dinner at McDonalds.

Prior to this episode, I will have to take this space and time to acknowledge the fact that John-Mark and I were so blessed to have Deacon Allison Owens to help us drive here, with the blessings of his wife...Bertha [we claim cousins]. They, along with other members of my church family, were very concerned about my moving here alone. It was indeed God's hand that covered me, because I became sick with bronchitis, and was in no condition to deal with an excited and active child! Deacon Owens' presence here for a few days also gave me a chance to get adjusted to the sounds of the house [every house has them.] I sure appreciated the much needed help with my son, as well as having a familiar face around in a new place! He kept John-Mark busy, among other things, he was teaching him how to be creative. They took a branch off of the big cedar tree out front, found a globe that fits over a light bulb and put the little Christmas tree inside...finding ribbons in the basement which became the decorations for it. I said, "This proves what we can do with a little of nothing!" It was a neat idea. This is what Pastor Neal and Jacqui found, when they came later on that night.

Subsequently, I discovered that Jacqui attended Pastor Neal's Church. We went there several times, but I decided not to be a part of another small church because of the heavy demands and responsibilities that work two or three faithful people to the bitter end of tattered nerves!

Oh, yes! I know that was a tacky reason, when scrutinizing from the outside of the subject; but when you have struggled with work, sweat and tears for over fifteen years in one small church...emotional and spiritual exhaustion is inevitable. Consequently, teaching the Word of the Father...Son and the Holy Ghost is overwhelmed by administrating. I will not go any further with this; number one...it is my personal experience and opinion...secondly...the book is not about the shortcomings of small churches, nor my reactions to same.

Nevertheless, I decided to go 'Church shopping' and find one big enough for me to hide in the pews, [or under!] so, that no one would miss me; whether I came once a month—or none! Believe it or not, we found one, made to order...with the exception of **one thing**...Pastor Schrade is quiet proficient at remembering names—and to try and hide—would have been in vain...[because there were only a few Blacks attending his Church at the time...and the other peculiarity was; I wore ostentatious hats!] However, when we were leaving this particular Church, John-Mark said, "Momma, you don't have to look any further; because I have found my personal Church!" And I said, "Me too Son!" So, we started going there, but part of me wanted to go to Pastor Neal's Church because I knew that it was a fledgling, or could it have been years of indoctrination as a member of a small church?

Howbeit, while pondering this, my spirit was warring...'**Do you really want to hide in the Pews...or do you want to be an integral part of a working ministry?**' and of course, I wondered if I had enough strength left for the dedication it takes to be involved in this small church. In the meantime...I was awakened one morning...with 'Read Haggi."

I pondered over this momentarily, and thought, "What does this mean?" I didn't remember anything about Haggi—and ordinarily, would not find it interesting to read! But I read this Book in the Old Testament, several times, even highlighted the scriptures that seemed to be talking to me...and after musing over it while talking to the Lord; I interpreted them to mean—go back to the small church and work...because, summarily, God told Haggi to tell the remnants of people, to work on his house, the temple, and they were having a hard time because he blowed on their efforts to get ahead in their homes; while, they were letting his house go to waste. I said, "Oh my Lord...I believe you are telling me to go back and work!" **OH-h YES!!**

I got my heels to clicking, in a hurry!...dragging John-Mark by the neck [so to speak] kicking and screaming! Because when I hear the Lord, **or think I hear him,** I get a move on!!!

Later, by the way of Pastor Earline Neal, the Holy Spirit directed me into writing poetry of special messages. He started me out thru Pastor Neal's request to write a Church Credo or tenet...[if you will.] As I stated in my first book that she was the second person, who asked me to do this; even so, I still felt the same tinge of ineptitude for this job of significance; as I did for my former patron!

So, I prayed for the help of the Holy Spirit and we produced the "Amazing Grace"–but this was the first step inside the door that God was opening for me. Hence, the book "Turn of the Century of Divine Reflections" and numerous of invitations to recite in various places... Churches...NAACP Luncheons...Civic functions and other programs, et cetera. [I had no idea that it would involve this kind of activity.]

One day my friend, Barbara Charles, [who is very influential in pushing me out to be discovered...and, also, my friends Clemmie and William Hinton, who makes me feel, 'I got it going on!' / tee-hee-giggle/] and I went to the Theater in the Tamarack to hear a poet of renown. She turned to me and said, "I can see you up there, reciting your poems." I laughed at her and said, "Girl, I know that you don't mean that!" She said, "Yes, I do. You can do just as well, or better!"...I just grinned in unbelief and said, "Unh-Unh!" But I had underestimated this "Mover and Shaker!"

Tamarack is a beautiful building designed in a circle, with an Oriental flair. It is a great tourist attraction and has unusual products made by the West Virginians that you cannot find anywhere else...which includes odd furniture pieces, and, also, houses the Hulett C. Smith Theater, where historical events are shown; plays performed, and poets recite on stage. Well, a year later, guess what? Her prophecy, indeed, came true, while standing there, reciting–I was waiting to come out of the dream.

My friend Jacqui, called me up one day, to tell me that she had gone to a community meeting and submitted my name to be on a program for a poetry recital in Beckley's Shoemaker Square, a City Park in downtown Beckley–a quaint place...reminiscence of the early nineteen hundreds–something one may see in the movies, or read about. The green lawns, shrubbery and big tree extend from the courthouse to the piazza, [opened space covered with cobblestones/bricks]–with a big gazebo that's used by the entertainers.

There is a variety of activities on "Fridays in the Park" day–for example, frying chicken wings–making sandwiches/hot dogs–drinks/ice cream...simultaneously, community interests are presented at designated tables...[just like old time movies!] I can imagine back in the twenties and thirties that the women had on these big long dresses with a dozen petticoats–accessorized with colorful bonnets and some with aprons–laid with starch! And the men wearing baggy black pants and white shirts opened at the neck–sporting black derby hats...maybe some wore big checker caps–cocked to one side and others were worn on the back of their heads. As I recited with the music blasting loudly; I felt that it was all an illusion, and wasn't really happening!

However, I sure gave the recital my best shot!!! A little old lady confirmed by coming up to me saying, "Miss...I sure enjoyed your **preaching**!" [heh-heh! I told you!]

I am, slowly, beginning to see why the Lord led me back to this small church. It isn't just for **one** thing. Surely, the spiritual relationship would not have materialized through the process of time; between Jacqui and me. We enjoy some spiritual depths in the revelation of the Word, because we both seek the truth beyond traditionalism. She is another blessing on my path. We are supportive of each other through prayers of encouragement and the WORD–during the low times and high times. Often, she shares musical tapes and videos on interesting religious subjects.

I should mention, the Pastors Earline and Roosevelt Neal, do not preach and teach **traditional messages**. We have been privileged to spiritual growth, exceedingly, under their tutelage. Their teaching of the in depth 'Word'...provokes thought and a real seeking of God, the Lord Jesus–the Holy Spirit and their relationship to us as the Holy Family, which takes us beyond...**just being 'Christians'**...but children, of the God family who nurtures us. So, you see; I would have missed this personalized teaching and the opportunity to exercise this great gift that the Holy Ghost has manifested in me. They have, for the past two years, allowed me to use the Church for a "Night of Poetry."

On one such occurrence, a friend came up to me, crying, she said, "I love you and I want to thank you for leading me back to the Lord, where I am going to stay."...and I assured her that I couldn't take the credit, because it was the work of the Holy Spirit! Oh!–I was so moved by this; it was indeed the confirmation of the presence of the Holy Spirit! And other spiritual incidents and comments sprang from this particular program. I just praised Him there, under the shadow of his hand!

After one of my recitals, on another occasion; a little boy approximately eight years old, no more than ten' came up to me and said, "Miss–I sure enjoyed your poetry!" and I thanked him, graciously. However, I am thinking, 'The words were big and powerful, and would have more meaning to an older child or a matured listener; yet he enjoyed it! And apparently, he got the message!' Tears welled up in my eyes, as I choked them back!

The Holy Spirit made another supernatural move, but this time I was shopping at the Wal-Mart Store, here in Beckley when Vanessa Thompson, who I had met at the Church of God Worship Center, came into the delicatessen department, where I was trying to make up my mind about which part of the chicken did I feel like eating–the breast?–the tendons?–the livers? Finally, I felt that I was being stared at, and there was...a quiet hush–as I looked around, a lady was staring at me, grinning and everyone was looking at her. Suddenly, I realized that it was Vanessa, and of course, we joyfully greeted each other with a hug. We were briefly exchanging small talk and then she called to her friend to introduce me. Vanessa started out with, "I want you to meet Henrietta Davison–she is one praying woman!...Henrietta, this is my friend, Annette Fox." Then she asked what had I done since we last met and I told her about my Book of Poetry that I had written. All of a sudden, the two started talking real fast; saying something about helping to get me publicized–and I–? my head was going back and forth, trying to fathom what was happening here! At last, they noticed that I was looking puzzled and Vanessa explained to me that Annette was a News Reporter at Herald Register and that she would do a write up on me. So we exchanged telephone numbers–and I left them in a sweat...[private summer had been activated!!] thinking, "This is surreal and what I just heard couldn't not have any truth in it–must be a tease!"

Approximately a week later, as I listened to my answering service, Annette was saying that she would like to set up an appointment with me; and I was thinking, "No, I'm not going any further with this–if it's real, what must I say–do? Oh...I can't! Oh Lorr-dd!" I kept saying, "How can this be happening to me–who am I? Certainly, not anybody important!" I just kept walking up and down in disbelief. Then after settling down a bit–first, I had to decide to call her back–secondly, if I were to follow through, what would be the best time? What the heck...I **had** to see this thing through! I **had** to go around the bend in the road! Yes, I made the call; though it took a lot of courage. We agreed upon a date and time.

On this particular date, the weather was very hot...the old truck that I was driving...didn't have air conditioning and along with my own private summer [Aw–you know! Do I have to spell it out?]...**I was very hot**; I was steaming like a stewed prune! So, when I arrived there at the Newspaper Office; I was like an overcooked noodle–sweating–[**not a oozing, but a gushing!**]...I'm talking about a **meansweat**! "Oh, thank God, I am here, early," I thought, "Now, I will have a chance to cool down! No such luck, no sooner than I had sat down–wiping running water from my face; Ms. Fox came out to invite me into the interviewing booth...Thinking and puffing. "Oh goodness, my clothes are clinging to my body!" As I got up to go in, "How can I look dignified like I have it all together? What is she going to say to me...what am I going to say to her?" Of course, Ms. Fox is very professional, she immediately put me at ease; however, as I sat down; I apologized, profusely, about my saturated appearance. She began to question me about my book and how my subject matter for poems were chosen. I began to remember what led me into each one. Guess what? More water fell! I cried all through the interview; asking forgiveness, as we talked. No, your imagination is not running away with you...I was one **soggy sister**!!!

Nevertheless, Ms. Fox, indeed, wrote the article and made me feel like a celebrity!! In the interview I had told her another book was in progress; since, it's out in the universe, I must complete this book!

The most rewarding and spiritual phenomenon, was how the Holy Spirit had taken control of this interview and manifested it into a wonderful experience. However, my part of the job was to **'press'n'sweat'**!

Subsequently, I sent the article in the newspaper to one of my sisters in Texas; and one day, I was checking my answering service and the lady was saying that she had read the article and wanted to know how to obtain one of the books. She left her telephone number and the name sounded familiar. I called and started by asking, "Are you my sister?" and she said, "Yes, I believe I am!"–Well, needless to say, I was overjoyed to hear from this sister, because I had not talked to her since my son, Barry, had died approximately four years ago. I believe, at that time, we had promised to keep in touch. The first family moved (my siblings and I) from the state of Texas, while we were quite young and over the years we, somehow, faded out of touch except for times of tragic events. I think this happens too often in many families.

She asked me to send her a book and to my chagrin–"Oh my Lord! I left out my second family of siblings and had not included them with the first siblings in by book! Oh–how could I have omitted them?"...in a state of being mortified, I concluded that it was an underhanded trick of the enemy; designed to bring about family hostility and division. I believe Satan's plan was to discourage the family reunion that he knew was coming forth from this renewed contact, which will be our family's first.

A DECREE OF BLESSINGS
For the Lighthouse Realty
Father...Bless This Business...Protect
AND

Let the beacon from the Lighthouse Realty...
be a ray of hope for them...who strives to enjoy the goodness...
of God's prosperity...

Let it be a light to every home that's sold...
presenting personable warmth...honesty and integrity.

Let the signs of the business be a trademark of distinction...
That's indicative of excellence—and worthy of recompense.

Let the rays beam!!!...as it transmits and emanates the highest of self-esteem...
to those who achieve...their cherished...dreams!!!

Let the Lighthouse Realty...be a guiding tower...deserving those...
who seeks the headiness...of ownership power.

Let the Lighthouse Realty...be a reflection of you, Father...while the
Godly principles of this business is applied...and practiced...
by not embracing the character...of unscrupulous tactics...

Let the 'byword' of the Lighthouse vanes...personify faithfulness...
loyalness...steadfastness and stalwartness...that's forever moving by
the directions...of the Lord Jesus Christ!!!

Let the Holy Spirit be the guiding light...
leading you to the highways and byways; while in the darkness of
night...

Let it be done Father, as to your will...bless this business and help
her till...so that it may have far reaching tentacles...
    extending...even...to the highest pinnacle...
As it embraces and flows with your love...
    through Anita Thomas...and to the clients that she serves!!!

A ROSE

One of thirteen children...
    was this special rose...caught up in the wind...
and scattered about...
    directed on another route...
life had dished out–a terrible plight...
    their mother's life–God did rescind...
and chose for her...another family to send...who was structured
    and strong–whose name was Wright!

Being relocated on a ten acre farm with a diversity of animals–that
    the family stocked...
beginning with dawn- and ending at dusk...
almost toiling–around the clock...
tugging and tusseling was hard labor–not easily savored!
but best not complain–and forget the fuss ---
    about body pains–and sore muscles...
cause 'back talk' -- they wouldn't take...
    and very unwise for your own health's sake.

The constant thought was –how to get this burden off her back...
Ah! Ha! Marriage is the answer...and in this thinking...
    ...emerged "Brack"...
had to move swiftly and not tarry...

For on this path...she was sharing...
burden and hardship...they...would carry...and –Ah-h-h –love...
but after the uniting -- there were bickering and biting –
    and unforeseen things...inclined to disturb...that cause their
marital tensions...to heighten.

Borne into this union were -- three girls and one boy
    Not leaving time...for too much joy...
The fun time had to be scrapped...had to go to work...an
economical rap earned between three marriages...with her "Brack"
The sentence was twenty years of slaving...working at hard labor --
there at Douglas Air Craft!

Even so–this Rose triumphed thru trials...of ups and downs...thistles
and thorns.
It continues to blossom and bloom with eighty years of power...
which it radiantly resumes as the rose of roses...with roots chosen
for its tenacity and...sweetness...that has no rival!

Still being capable and able to transcend time...leaving a beloved
spirit–trailing behind...embedding it in the membrane of her
family –and into all who have lingered...in the sweet essence –of
her presence!!

"A Rose" was written by special request from Joyce Duren-Seabrook
for her Mother's 80th birthday, where she journeyed to California to
share in the joyous occasion with Mrs. Willie Duren.

A Dedication to: Willie Duren

Happy! Happy!! Eightieth Birthday!!
@ May 17, 2001

ABOVE THE WORLD

Above the world is where everyone would like to go...
A place where dreams come true and no man–says "No."
This place that I speak of–is better than a high...
for each step, you take–you feel light as a fly.

Above the world is an escape from sin. You will never lose, but
forever win. And for pleasure –you will feel the best –nothing can
explain –but it's better than the rest. For at night, you can watch the
stars from the other side...for luxury –find a cloud and take a ride–
and anywhere –you'll be free to go–no one can stop you –and no
one can say, "No!"

Above the world is an echo of joy–they match each other like a
kid's toy–and all the happiness may be found there. No more sad
days and no more fear. For the weather is like spring time all year
round–and no one can explain the feeling of love that is found. So
when hope runs low and times get hard–take a flight to–above
the world!!

Author, Clarence Garland

CRUCIFIED

To save the world –Jesus
     died...
Put on the Cross to be–
     crucified.

The guard pierced Him in his
     sides...
Blood and water gushed–
     as He died
and He was spat upon–also, reviled...
as they cast lots for His clothes...
     laying in a pile.
Nails made big holes in His hands–
     and feet
while He hung there–in pain and–
     grief...
finally, crying out–seeking relief
"My God! –My God! –why hast thou–
forsaken me?

And oh-h the blood that was running–
     Down...
splattered upon us–as it flowed to the
     ground;

buying us with the premium price–
of Jesus divine and holy life!!

On the third day Jesus did
       arise...
and after forty days–while the disciples gazed...a cloud came to
take him–away...then quicker than light–He moved out of their
sight!–
Across the skies–to our Father's side;
where He reigns–and is very much–alive!!

We will all be gathered,–one day soon...
to be raptured up–to meet our groom...
where our dwelling–is prepared in heaven above –
       with real joy–peace and love...
There,...we'll forever rest and abide...
In a mansion –build just for us–to reside.

DEAR PASTOR AND WIFE:

As we journey through
       this life...
the years pass by...oh, so fleetly;
leaving cherished memories...
of the good and the bad times that entwined,
which has served to bond us more
       completely.

Pastor J.W. Range...Missionary Isadora Range
       You both were assigned a task...
how hard is the travel...how heavy is the burden
       you did not ask.

But you took God's hand
       and made a stand...
and then you joined the Christian Band.

You both knew that the road
       would not be easy...
And that you faced more heat than gentle
       breezes...
But you held on to the faith and believed...
       that God's servants...He never leaves.

Any so my Pastor–and "Mama Queen"
      you toil and tug–behind the scenes...
it is too late now, to turn around, it seems;
because there are still many souls left...
      needing guidance...to God's mainstream.

These were nine years...in God
      you trust...
the call on your lives–have been the...
      service and benefit for all of us...
as you performed your Christian duties...
      joyously and justly.

GOD'S PLATIMUM SOLDIERS

We are God's Platinum Soldiers
as we move to and fro...
we prance and shuffle...our feet to the music...
and when we dance–our spirits flow
shuffling the right foot to the left...rhythm moves...
improves our steps -...dancing for the Lord's joy–...and yours–
while shining like platinum and pure gold.

Come on now...move your feet   --   and work your toes...
let loose–so the spirit flows
cause God's Platinum Soldiers...
dance with the heart...in the midst   --   of their souls.

We dance to the tempo beat–
like wings–on our flying feet–
me move in harmo-ny...per-fecting unity...
glorifying God and magni-fying...these are the ways–
we express our praise.

David...a mighty king...who reigned
put down his scepter–and bared himself...
to dance and sing before the Lord...
as he praised...His holy name.

We are God's Platinum Soldiers...
and David is chosen...as our model...
singing and dancing...swinging our bodies...
in a sacrifice of praise.

Onward we dance...God's Platinum Soldiers...
praising the Lord–with swirling scarves...
worship-ing Him...as a spiraling collage.

God's Platinum Soldiers is on the march...
on the spiritual path...we go...
we use dancing and singing...as our arch...
to lift the spirit...of depressed souls.

God's Platinum Soldiers is on the run
God's Platinum Soldiers is dancing on...
God's Platinum Soldiers face -- a new dawn...
we'll run–sing–and dance–to a beginning–just begun!!!
Because we are–God's Platinum Soldiers!!! [Yeah–Hurray!!]

HEAR THE BABY CRYING!!

Sh! Sh! Sh! A baby is crying
Listen! But, wait!
The sounds are different
there are several cries...
each voice is distinctive—as it multiples.

Harken! Do you hear it?...A host of babies—all in one...
sounds seem to be coming—out of this little town...
all of the earth is delivering—a universal birth.

The stars are leaping—the moon is luminous in the night...
the sun is radiant—with its dancing light!!
There is an excitement in the air—while all living
creatures begin to travel—hoping to be the first greeters -
to make it there.

While moving towards the cries—of travail;
they were aware—at the height of the walls...
that an unusual phenomenon—was taking place.

The voice of many babies—in one cry...but no one
understands—the reason why!
Could it be an unusual birth—in the universe? Are we reshaped in
the 'spirit womb'—and delivered thru the loins of the newborn—
waiting to be reborn!!!

A strange cry that alerts–all ears to hear...
as it draws everyone near...
where is the child? where is the mother?
The sounds are like no other...where is the place...we need to see
this child's–face!!

Let's check the hospitals–homes and clinics–motels–hotels–and
Traveler's Inn.
Even Old Herod is sending his men–to find this child and bring him
in!!

But there is a great hush...only the elect could hear...as they gathered
around–to listen to the sounds...
ready to confirm the prophetic time–for the moving of the
Holy Spirit–upon mankind.

Sh! Sh! Hear the baby's wails–of poignant yearnings in a world
that's speedily plunging–into a dark chasm–of no returning.

I hear Jesus saying–"I will be their Savior -- Father...I will be their
Living Water...I am He–who will descend from above–into this
world–as one like them...because these are our children–of whom
I love."

Listen, hear the angels singing? They are all rejoicing!
Happiness is resounding...in their voices!
The prophets' predictions of a Savior being born–came down thru
generations–of the prophetic horn.

Mary was chosen for the supernatural birth...
Joseph...God's selection for the Father role–on earth...

Jesus was embraced by his Mother's arms–and smiling charm–
As–He was guided by a Father–who kept him from harm...
taught how to work–even in dirt...and instructed from his youth–
how to use his hands...being led and directed in the footsteps
of a man...and after this was attained...his Heavenly Father
took the reins.

Now,...He had to be–spiritually trained.
It was time, for the prophecy–to be fulfilled...which–from the
 beginning–was his role.
And his Heavenly Father's ultimate goal–
 for him to die on the cross to redeem man's soul.
At this very moment...He's at his Father's right hand side...
In heaven–He presently resides...
And while the angels are singing...all around!!!
He stands–King of Kings–Lord of Lords...and more than worthy–
to wear His Crown!!

"I HAVE LOOKED FOR YOU"

I wrote this poem approximately thirty-five years ago, and while going through and reading my repertoire of poems; I compared my feeling then, with today's.

It is amazing! At that time, I was feeling unloved...emotionally abused...depressed and in deep gloom...in other words "the pits!" and was wondering if there was anyone out there alive, who would fit the descriptions of whom I seeked in the poem. Even though, I was married; it certainly was not my mate, however, I had made the choice,... but he didn't "fit the bill" [old adage] of a loving husband...he was about things...big gifts–but not of himself.

During this time, my children were older teenagers...bucking at the 'bits' like mules...stubborn, obstinate...trying to be adults before time! Yet, expected me to take care of their necessities; you know... like food, clothes, and a decent place to live...and Oh! Don't forget!... they had to have transportation...**'looking good' transportation**! They called it "**Styl-l-ing**! And these were years ago. Today's children are the same; it's a vicious cycle–that continues. It was about, 'Mother, make it happen'...'Mother, help me'...'Mother, it's about me; not you'...'Well, Mother, you only need to take care of **our** needs'...don't worry–**leave our lives to us**!

Well, this is a little background of what was going on in my life...and mind. I was also recuperating from major surgery, which made me feel helpless; like a worn out and unwanted garment.

It is comprehensible, to fantasize about a loving, gentle and sweet 'Prince Charming'; who would lift me up from my despondency. So, in this highly emotional state of mind; I wrote this poem. However, much later; [today] it has become apparent that I was describing the presence of the "Holy Spirit"–through Him. Now, I need not look any further!!! **Praise the Lord!!!!**

I HAVE LOOKED FOR YOU

I have looked for you–
in my dreams–
I have looked for you–
In the words of a song– I have looked for you–
in the melodies of sweet music.

Ah, yes! I have looked for you in the spring time–
when the birds are singing, the flowers are budding;
the earth is bursting...with verdure and everything is
coming alive–fresh as a new birth I looked for you...
and became discouraged.

As my spirit grieved in disillusion...the tears were held captive
in stifled bonds...while my heart mumbled...in forlorn...
then...suddenly!! like a flash of lighting and bolt of thunder–
I found you!...no longer...will I be confused!

You are everywhere...and in everything...that is alive...
that is gentle...that is soft and melodious...that is comforting–
like a warm blanket around me...like a cool breeze in a summer
evening...like the sweet smell of spring time...like sweet music
and a sip of new wine–where we meet in the true vine...
there at the end of an arduous and...frustrating day...with love...
we indeed...dine!

IN REMEMBRANCE OF MOTHERS

Mothers, who are an extended conduit -
for carrying and
deliverance of life...
and from the baby's first cry– Mother's hear– until she dies...
walking the floor all thru the night–seemingly no relief in sight!
But finally, the little tyke starts growing up–"to the terrible twos"!–
where everything good–he refuses!

Then the child grows to be a few inches taller–becoming a
    teenager– who swaggers...
a bouncing walk–with hipless clothes bagging...a snarling mouth
spouting vitriolic words–shooting back and forth–like daggers.

Mothers hear the cry of puberty and screaming hormones -
    while seeking God's face and grace–with tearful
moans–"Oh when will this child be grown?"

Well, finally, the child is gone–to college– to work– to service–
to the streets– to anywhere...**just gone**!!!
And then our moans turn into groans– real serious business, now -
is on!!
The floor walking–when they were babies–has turned into worry -
    and tearful pacing...

Loudly! We call on God–Jesus–Holy Spirit–and the Host of
    Angels...to watch over– them...
We pray for comfort thru His grace–while we sing soulful hymns...
and when the level of their lives change...sometimes with pain–
Mothers elevate to another suffering realm...**and**
From the cradle to your grave–they're on your heart...even–if you
out live them–their presence is still a part–of your memory chart–
as it was–right from the start!!

NO LEAD—HOT LEAD

I once knew a person that got shot in
his head;
and a child in school with a pencil
without any lead;
not following the rules...because he was busy...
acting a fool...
so he got a gun and took it to school...because he thought
he was cool;
so he went to the classroom and pointed his gun...
pumping hot lead...
because he had nothing in his head...no lead in his pencil; so he
wanted to...
be dead!!

By John-Mark Davison

NO WORDS

[Expressions of Impressions; after the demise of

my husband on March 9, 1988]

There are no words
To describe...
having friends by your side when, suddenly, a part of
your life goes out
and leaves you stumbling about.

There are no words
to describe...
when a hand is felt...a word of love is heard
and a prayer...
all of this says...a friend is there.

There are no words
to describe...
the observance of food being prepared...sitting in the quietness of
someone's presence...or maybe there is a call...
just to say...a friend is here...who cares.

There are no words...
to describe
a loss...a hurt...a separation...

or a part left from a whole...
an aching heart or a...
mourning soul.

There are no words
to describe...
when the heart is at its heaviest and God lifts the weight...
bringing comfort and peace to a
restless state.

There are no words
to describe...
the feel of God on your side...
or to have family and friends when in grief...you can confide...
who are ready to share their strength...when you decide.

There are no words
to describe...
my church family...who has been so precious...
lifting me up...out of deep depressions
I love you...I thank you...I thank you...I love you!!

"O' MY GENTLE BREEZE"

O' My Gentle Breeze was written in the early sixties, when I was going through some family problems [see excerpts of "I Looked For You]. I was recuperating from surgery and I was remembering how nice my Doctor was to me [I will **not, either**–name him!] We would have little chats [we both smoked] as we indulged in our smoking habit. Funny thing, I really didn't like him at first. I thought he was too, fine looking [well...down right handsome!] for such a serious job as my surgery. He popped in my room, while I was settling in; I thought, he was an attendant, or something, until he introduced himself as being my Doctor! I was sarcastic, because he was just, too, handsome and "ditty-boppish" [cocky] to be a Doctor! Besides, I had my own personal problems and didn't need another aggravation...like a 'cocky Doctor'!!

After the surgery was over, he would come in to check on my improvement–you know, just medical talk...I really don't know when the conversations got into personal talk about my unhappy domestic situation and I started to look forward to the chat...because the visit from my mate was few and far in between...'that's another story!]. I want clarity here, though, my Doctor never led me on! And I never let on about my feelings changing; I was just, too much of a lady for that! [besides, I was quite shy...and wouldn't have been able to deal with further rejection] In retrospect, I was not aware of it myself–until I came home to a 'chill'... only to be compared with a day of winter in Beckley!

I called my friends together, and I read the poem that I had written to my Doctor because they were always there to support me down through the years...'hold my hands, so to speak'. We seriously discussed this situation...[like job and his compatriots] and I was in a tizzy, and determined to present this poem. Afraid?...Yes!! But I had to see what was around the bend!

Soon, I had an appointment for a follow-up. I had, previously, asked him to be my outpatient Doctor, but his office didn't take my insurance. [I felt like changing mine!] because I couldn't follow him as a regular patient. The Holy Spirit saved me from a dastardly mess! Satan was setting me up, by using the turmoil in my life to slay me physically, mentally and emotionally! Woe would have been me!!

However, I kept my appointment, and finally, I got up enough nerve to present the poem, which he read, while I was sitting there–so-o chagrined!! There were many things, he could have said or done–but he was very chivalrous and explained that he was flattered; he said when I heal, the feeling that 'I think' that I had, would dissipate. He said that this often happens, when there are family problems and these types of feelings are called transference...of course, I, have actually forgotten the psychological terms that he used. Nevertheless, "O' My Gentle Breeze" is apropos to his persona. In my vulnerability, he had the power at hand, to undermine my self-esteem for life! Was he right! I don't know, even now, I have a special softness for him...perhaps, because he was there, when I needed a carrying person...and, also, he was so gentle in handling this delicate matter! Hum-m, I wonder where you are today?

O' MY GENTLE BREEZE

When did it all begin–this new awakening??
When did it begin–this fervor to be fulfilled?

How will it end? This anxiety of not knowing how
to begin–to either quell this madness -
   or to release this foreign passion
that has been ignited–by your gentle touch...
   'O' My Gentle Breeze!!'

Tell me my thoughts are childish...
You–tell me that this phase of my life...is mere frustrations...
   that will dissolve into yesterday...
and become memoirs of tomorrow.

Yes,–tell me you are an insignificant fantasy, which will
never materialize–and that I will only find...
   in my shallow mind...
'O' My Gentle Breeze!'

THE LOVE OF LIFE

Never enough time...never enough knowledge...
   never enough wisdom...or time for fun...
never enough energy...as we walk thru life's–journey
never enough creations to be made...in just one more–day
but there is always the Hope–that keeps us striving...
   just one more hour...
and we will conquer all of the 'NEVERS'–when our fears are
gone...
Cause we Never-Ever...have to walk Alone.

When the road is rocky–slip on your easy sneakers...
   you can walk- tho' a little warbly...
When it is dark–use your high beam flashlight...
   press forth to your goal–press positive to your mark!
Use your special compass–don't be downcast...
Jesus is all of these that you need–and much–much more!

When we feel that we can no longer go on -
We can't–but He can!! --- and–He will!
Call on Him–be still...His presence will be revealed...
Trust Him and He'll direct you–through...
Cause we are NEVER too bad–NEVER too wicked...
NEVER too rotten–vile...nor vicious...
   enough to make Him mad...

He just uses these ingredients–to shape us into better creatures!
This we can NEVER do ourselves!

God gave us Life...and loves us as His Life...
gave His Son's Life...to save our life...
He is the epitome–of Love and Life
So, under our own power we need not -
Strive!! But with free will–flow in the highest power
of the truest and purest of love–every hour...
allowing our souls to be immersed–restored–and filled!

THE STOPPING OF THE CLOCK

The hands on the clock moves with precision,
back and forth the pendulum whizzes,
until–finally–a sudden decision;
to stop the clock while life dismisses...

The moving hands continue to turn–
with a steady hourly chime,
and our lives–too, revolving–
right with the Clock's time...

But the length of life is Gold's concern,
to begin and end --- His will be done...

So, our time should be spent–
harvesting spiritual fruit,
leaving none behind– for Satan to recruit!
and if we stay strong– we can surely block,
His evil wiles– before God
stops the Clock...

Our ultimate goals in life–
before we go,
should be new heights– on the spiritual plateau...
so, let's stop the moaning and groaning
and the tears that drop,

and prepare to meet the Maker ---
before He stops the Clock,
by ending our life– to the tolls
of the last tick tock!
TICK TOCK! Tick Tock! tick tock!

THE VISITOR
Knock! Knock! Knock!

Who the hell is it knocking at my door; at 12 o'clock midnight?

It is I, Mr. Death, and I hope your soul is right.

Mr. Death? Oh no!...Well it must be a mistake; did you check your records? I'm only 28!

Yes I did, my records show, "It's time for you to go."

But if you take my soul, I'll never see my son turn 8 years old.

Well...you should have thought about that 8 years ago.

Mr. Death, I know there's something you can do!

I'm sorry, I just collect the souls, there is a higher source that you need to talk to.

Oh my! I haven't talked to my Lord in over a year; now, you suggest that I call Him...when I'm in fear?

Look! Normally, it takes me three seconds a soul, but dealing with you, makes it hard to do what I'm told!

I'll grant you a few more precious strokes of this thing, you call time...and believe me; I never forget those souls that I've left behind!

I'll grant you a day or a year...one wish I will select...but, when I come the second time around...your soul, I will collect!
I leave you with a heart attack; to let you know how precious time can be, because whether you like it or not, one day, you have to see me!!

Clarence D'Wayne Garland

WHAT IS LOVE

[A farewell–to the Church of God, PGT, in Altadena, California and
my friends...when we moved here to Beckley]

What is love...but your family and friends...
being there for you when trouble begins and
lingering with you–unto the end.

What is love–other than the overwhelming feeling of–warmth that
embraces and emanates from us–as we interact with one another.

What is love–but an expression without words–and holds without
arms and hands...that lets you know–we are one with the universe–and
we all are family.

What is love...except giving without the need for returns–in joy–sad-
ness–happiness–troubles–sickness or health...including the heart that
beats as one with yours–fortified and channeled into a singular beat–
that makes us one with God.

What is love...but sharing and caring–a burden to lighten–a smile to
share–a prayer– with someone, who is always...there.

Love is– all of these things that I am witnessing and feeling here
tonight– and much–much more...enough to fill volumes of books–with
a world of words– still unsaid.

Our absence will be presence with you in the spirit...you can never be replaced in our hearts–nor do we wish you to be.
However, we will be as close as your telephone...and our residence for visiting.

Your love–we will carry like a warm robe...wrapped around us, tightly– as our security blanket; while we go through our adjustment period... because your love is our comfort–on this journey of–uncertainty.

I am elated to have this second chance to rectify this omission; which was perpetrated by an evil force–the enemy of all families, Satan, who initiated his warfare, in the Garden of Eden...with Adam and Eve.

I am taking great pleasure in presenting, Vonceille Roberson Mardell Loyd, Christine Henderson, Gayle Henderson and William Henderson, Jr....These are my sisters and brother from the second family, whose mother is Mae Dell Henderson, and as a youth; I spent many enjoyable times with them. At this point, I will also give honorable mention to my sister-in-law, [brother, K. Willard's wife] Everlean, an incredible person, who is very dear to me.

There are other cherished people in my church family here in Beckley...Alma Logan, who has been so wonderful to me. She has taught me so much about my computer, picking up where my friend, Kathy Lousteau, left off in California. She shares computer information and picks me up for church; when I am mechanically stranded, and is so encouraging and helpful with my Poetry Programs. I just thank God for this beautiful woman put in my life. There is my other loving sister, Rosa [Rosarita, I like to call her] who has, likewise, been very kind to me.

I must acknowledge another dear person, Apostle Doris Wicker; who during my first writings, was kind enough to invite me to her church to do a recital. I did "God Pointed His Finger" and He truly blessed. Later on, she invited me to her church banquet at the Holiday Inn to do a recital; I did a sequel of poetry, which God gave favor. Pastor Wicker has since married Bishop Fred Adams, a likeable, lively and vibrant man.

As I was writing this introduction, I got a call from Sister Jacqui requesting a recital in [a new place for me] here in Beckley, at the "Soldier's Memorial." [WOW]! "Sister Solider" sees that I don't become stagnant! Later, the 'Mover and Shaker' told me that I may have the opportunity to recite on the Radio!!! [do you believe this?] I got an instant headache!...It was just too much excitement! I have been wanting to put "The Lying Beast" out in the air for eons!

WWNR 620 AM and WCIT 103.7 FM Radio Station in conjunction with the Crossroads Mall sponsored the 'Awards Night' for Ten Black Leaders of Beckley, in honor of Black History Month. What a privilege to serve as "Mistress of Ceremony" and to recite "Am I My Brother's Keeper" on the program. [it's in this Book]. It was ironic, I had previously met the General Manager of the Radio Station, Jay Quesenberry and his wife, Janet...very lovely people.

I think it is worthy to note, Janet and I had met via telephone; she was checking her telephone ID numbers, being in a rush to go out [someplace], I assured her that I had no knowledge, 'could it have been my son, who made the call?", I asked. Somehow, we started talking and she began telling me about her illness, and I am in this hurry–even putting on clothes as we talked...but the Holy Spirit had me to slow down and listen, and pray for her–and of course, I did!! I never thought of meeting this lady, ever in life, but I did! It was awesome! We have since been at some of the same functions...and, matter of fact, I had recited "Hear the Babies Crying" [it's in this book] in the home of our friend-in-common at her Christmas party, which Jay commented, favorably and Janet bought my book.

Nevertheless, the grand slammer of February 26, 2002 at the 'CROSSROADS MALL' was exciting! [On my Pilgrimage, every '**First**' is a stimulus!] I WAS ESTATIC!!! [I was afraid!] My sister, friend and prayer buddy, Joyce Seabrook, and I pray, hardily, for my calmness. When she is present we pray before I go on program–then I appear as if "I am cool as a pea!" "Got it going on!" and all of the other applicable cliché's. She is so precious...a gentle soul with a gentle spirit–who has time for everyone. I felt awful, calling her for transportation these past three or four weeks. Everybody wants a piece of her time and I can see that it's very draining...BUT she shares! and shares! and shares!... because she is such a caring person.

Before leaving this stage of my book I feel that I must expound, further, on the goodness of my Father, who brought me here to Beckley. He placed me in the midst of the most beautiful neighborhood of neighbors that one dreams and reads about-similar to neighborhoods of yester years; which reminds me of the TV show "Mr. Rogers' Neighborhood" for children.

I could write a book about them, certainly an inspired poem, and I just might; one of these days.

However; for the sake of not "changing horses in the middle of the stream" [I know everyone has heard this old adage], "I will keep my words to a minimum." My neighbors that live across the street from me, Darrell and Dixie Stegel have been so hospitable to us. Once, I had a big smoke coming from my basement furnace [I was a novice at making a fire] I didn't know what to do with the house smoking and me choking. I didn't think it was bad enough to call 911 because there was no blaze; so my next alternative was to call them, [either way, I felt quite foolish!] but they came right over. Mr. Stegel lit the paper that I had stuffed in the furnace and brought their fan over to help blow out the smoke. They stayed with me until everything was under control. In the winter months, Mr. Stegel shoveled snow from my walkway so I could get to my mailbox and Mrs. Stegel always reminds me not to stay over here in need–just call them.   Oh, they have done much more for John-Mark and me! I hold them high in God's eyes, in my prayers, while I praise and thank Him for my neighbors.

My neighbors up the hill, to my right side; Dwayne an Darlene Cox, also helps us. During the winter months, when the snow was very heavy; they would take John-Mark and bring him back from the bus stop or school, so that I wouldn't have to come out. Especially, since the day (when it was my turn) to take the children to the bus stop, I started up the hill to pick up their son [there was no show]...but the car started bucking and turning the way it wanted or didn't want to go...I couldn't go forward or backward...I was one praying sister...unto this day, my getting back into my driveway is a complete blank!!!...I prayed so hard, the Holy Spirit had to have driven me back home!! After I found out about the black ice, I made up my mind **that day**...my boy would have to walk or go to school during the summer months! And I promised myself, when winter is in; I will test the ground by beating it with a stick, and if the stick flies back at me-like a karate chop I wasn't going any place...**that day**...**week**...**or month**!! I am so grateful to them...they made me welcome to call on them in the time of need. Mr. Cox, also, assists his son, Brandon, in mowing my lawn. Day and night, I hold these precious people up to the Lord, as I praise Him.

Living right in front of me, again, up the hill are Richard and Kim Cox. One day during the first winter months, after we moved here...I heard this noise out in my driveway, "What in the world is this?" I didn't know whether someone was coming to bulldoze us out, or what!!! [our first winter here] Cautiously, as we looked out, I couldn't believe my eyes! My neighbor, Mr. Cox was cleaning the snow off of my driveway! I didn't know him at the time, but later on, I put a "Thank You" card in their mailbox. However, this was just the beginning of our neighborly relationship. Mrs. Cox keeps a 'keen eye' out on my place. When we are out of town; or if she hasn't seen me in a while...I will either get a call, or she'll come down to see if I am alright. Once, when I was back home; [California] she called the police on some people that she thought was moving us out...saying, "Well, you hadn't told me you were moving, so I called 911! The police had my landlord in questioning, who was here re-doing the bathroom! I hold them high before the Lord's face; as I praise Him!

Another neighbor, Donna, has recently moved into our neighborhood; who is friendly and neighborly. I was delighted, when she came over during the Christmas Holidays and played some gospel songs on my piano. She said, "I love Black Gospel music!" And I said "Me too!" I hold her up and thank God for sending another good neighbor to live next door to me!

God picked my neighborhood...picked my neighbors, and surrounded me with these genuinely, caring people.

My list of friends continues to grow. I must mention that I met Jean Evansmore, by way of John-Mark...approximately, two years ago, when he invited her to come to our table and eat lunch with us and she accepted because she 'doesn't meet strangers, either.' Subsequently, we went to Orlando Florida to the AARP Convention. I wanted to see and hear Dr. Maya Angelou. I heard that our delivery style of poetry recital had some similarity, and I wanted to see and hear her; before I say "Thank you." It is indeed an honor to be compared to her, even though, I fall short. [I hear someone saying..."Un-hum way short!] **WAY short**?...I shall not put that out into the Universe. I don't want the Holy Spirit to do a reversal of the gift that he has manifested in me! Dr. Maya Angelou has a dynamic personality, which exudes love and spirituality! I would like to think that I, also, house these specific traits.

However, there was another treat; I saw Bill Cosby, who was hilarious!

Jean has since married Dr. Stuart Frazier, a very nice man, who I've added as an extension of her to my growing list of friends.

I met Anita Thomas in 1995, while on vacation here in Beckley. I called a real estate company because I wanted to explore some of the areas and a possible location to reside. My friend, Barbara Lousteau came with John-Mark and me; she said, "Since you won't change your mind, I am going with you because Henri...you are stubborn and got a head like a rock! You and this child don't need to be traveling that far alone!" She and I both fell in love with Beckley, it was so tranquil! She never took naps before we came here.

Anita came and spent the evening showing us around. Neither one of us had any idea that we would become close friends...even to the idea that John-Mark and I would be considered as extended family. We have enjoyed spending the Christmas Eves with her and the family. Her daughter, Lisa, is a beautiful, friendly, and charming young lady, who is in college and becoming a doctor.

Anita and my son Barry have the same birthday. It was so amazing that I had chosen a picture of a Lighthouse for his obituary–and when I came back home to Beckley–Anita had named her business... Lighthouse Realty. What a coincidence!

I bought an antique typewriter while I was visiting here and left it in Anita's care and told her that I would be coming back. Yes, she had it when I moved here!

One day she saw me and said, "I had planned on calling you...I want you to pray and bless my Realty's Open House"...and I thought "O' my Lord! She can't mean that!" [there are some people who can really 'belt' out a prayer...but I am just an ordinary 'pray-er' . however; I will never refuse to pray, if someone asks me...or if the Holy Spirit tells me to.] In this instance, I called on Him. I especially do this when I'm treading in unknown territory...so, He gave me a prayer poem that night; "A Decree of Blessings" for the Lighthouse Realty. Nevertheless, I tried to hide behind the 'belters', when she brought me into the group...but Anita turned sideways so she could beckon me with her big eyes, [a compliment; she has beautiful eyes!] to come forth when the Pastor and Minister had prayed. After my prayer, I led right into the poem. Seemingly, it resonated over the mountains and the interstate...[the ceremony was held outside] and then I presented the poem to her, which she says is always inspirational when she reads it. I have included it in this book. Since this beautiful event, she has married Mark...really nice man. He is added to my list of friends, as an extension of her.

Clemmie Hinton, my friend, introduced me to a young man, Clarence Owens, who is such a wonderful person. John-Mark had said, "Moms Dear...I need a man in my life to take me to games and go fishing." I said, "I know son, but I won't marry him for you!" So, I thought, "Let me find a big brother, quick!" I discussed this with Clemmie, she made the contact with Clarence and he came into our lives.

Clarence has helped me with putting programs on my computer, moving it upstairs...hauling junk for me to my antique shop [oops! I mean merchandise!]...taking John-Mark fishing, tutoring him in math and spending time with him. He never took a dime!!...No, **Not a red cent!!!** However, his name precedes him with his outstanding benevolence to his church...children and other people. He is an exceptional person. I even had the audacity to call him, to change the furniture around in my living room, during the holidays. He did it and as usual–with a pleasant attitude. I try not to bother him, unless I just have to. He doesn't talk 'goodness'...he just is! He is now teaching a computer class "free" in the evenings at his church after his regular work hours.

He was presented one of the awards to the ten Black Leaders in Beckley...although he wasn't there to receive it; at first I thought that he was being modest, but he had been notified too late to change his computer class. Now that's commitment!!!!

I quickly squash and discourage any "Diddy-Boppers" [don't ask me to define...it just came to me] from bouncing up in my face, calling me "Mother Davison"...but Clarence has earned, in my opinion, the right. [No, he doesn't call me Mother Davison]. However; sometimes I refer to him as my god-son. I don't say it around him...he is much too modest to hear me say that. He is a rare specimen, indeed!

He is now married to Cassandra...a lovely person with a sparkling personality. I have added her to my list of friends as an extension of my god-son. [God sure sent him to me and John-Mark].

Cindy, a dear friend that I met as my manicurist and still is as of today. I have followed her all over Buckley and even into another town. She has such a sweet spirit. It's not about my nails, but about visiting... quality conversations and friendship. I am never in a hurry when I go– neither is she rushing around. The atmosphere is calm and comfortable; we run from one subject matter to the other. She is a very caring person, kind and helpful. The Lord has blessed her business, tremendously. She has since married Adam Bostic, a good man, who I have added to my list of friends as an extension of Cindy.

Mary Harrison, another lovely, involved person, who I met through her friend, Barbara Charles.

I have recently met two other beautiful people, Ethel Bivins, who I call my "Running Buddy", and Carolyn Jones...both are vibrant and outgoing who are high powered professionals; whose support is demonstrative by their purchase of my book.

In acknowledgement to everyone who I have "touched upon" during my journey, perhaps there was not a name...or perhaps it was so, fleetingly,...a smile...or...???; I record in this book...with gratitude!

God has truly blessed my pilgrimage, here in Beckley, which I thought would be a "laid back in peace' and resting place for me. You know retirement in the true sense of the word...writing...and moving around every once and awhile. But-He's saying, [while I'm thinking..."No, No",] "I have more work for you to do...Don't you say you're **ageless**?" Consequently, He placed all of these beautiful-aggressive 'on the move' productive people on my pathway, to serve as a catalyst in this new era of my life.

I thank God for keeping me progressively
-----------------------------------:

"IN THE SHADOW OF HIS HAND!"

Signs of the

Times

SIGNS OF THE TIMES

Lord~~we bow down low...at your feet...
Living day by day...in complete~defeat.
Wading in river of tears and trembling...
along with our peers.
Oh~h!!~~Let us see the reflection...
Of your Holy Face perfected...in this bloody place...

Flesh being torn with Evil hands...and knotted fists...
To make us swallow the lying myth...
That it's a birthright~~God's gift...
To turn a brother's life~into a public stench...'
Slaughtering those~~without strength...
Executing the authority...of Willie 'the' Lynch~

Peel the flogged skin...and let it be flung~
On the root...where the noose hung~
From that tree...there~the neck swung...
Wild beast crouched...with mockery...
Under white sheets. Do you hear the laughter?...
Ah~h...Yes!...the preparation was made~~
For the leech...to enjoy the bloody treat.

Brothers against brother...is a concern...
When Biblical Scriptures are search...and confirmed...

That the role of jealousy...and its kind...
Is an evil force...that controls...
As it detonates the body...And obliterates the soul!

Abel's blood is heard~from the earth...
Accusing Cain~of his murder...
And Joseph plea~for brotherly mercy...
Was ignored...as he was sold...
And put into...a deep dark hole.

Multitudes of black slaves~~and others~~
With no way to escape...the fanaticism~of power...
That enslaves bodies~minds~and emotions.
This evil stratagem was enforced...
to assure a future...Void of hope...
While heads bowed~to the dangling rope.

GO AHEAD!! Raging *mad dogs*...!!
Gnash-gnaw and slash with your claws...
Peel the bark from the back~of the 'ole tree...
Draw the bloody sap~with the bull whip and strap...
Rip the skin...open every wounded gap...
So that the garments can be attached~
As a reminder...to the 'Judgment Cap.'

Howl!!~tree roots...flooded with blood...
The mournful sounds are loudly~heard.
Cry!!~leaves of saturated and fearful tears...
Break...limbs!!...drop the necks~that's being stretched~~
Shake...and turn loose~noose...enough of your abuse!!
Lawd!...Lawd!! Wher yu bin?'
We struggl' and sputter blud...oin ebbur~en'!

The 'trocious wins~an' pow'ful foes~~
Twissing...us's to and fro~~
An lik de ank'shun tree~~fil wid blud~
Swet and teers...
We kant led go...
So' we'lla be holin' on to our roots~~widdout fears...
Prain' for de promis~~HOPE...whil we tris to cope.

The horror of mourning sounds and groans~
Still resonate today...Of yesteryear's lashing leather~~
And heads being bashed together.
Flesh...adhering to the bones~~hearts turning to stone...
Blood flowing~~Like surging waters...
Tears gushing~like flooding rain.
Oh~h!~ The excruciating pain!...only Jesus could sustain.

But`lest we forget...Nothing is to hard~~for God!
"We are his people and the sheep of his pasture"...
He is the Reaper with the Sickle~of what is sowed...
And our Book Keeper~~of what is owed...

Lord~~You were a long time coming...
But you were just over the hill...
Preparing Barack Obama~like David...
Was your Holy Will...
And each one of their Goliaths...
Were brought down to size...
Because a time for change...was recognized.

So~~Father God...with much stamina...
And political drama...
You led the people's heart...
To choose Barack Obama...

For the country's highest honor~and office...
Already "*Paid in full!!...by millions of coffins!*"
So-in the Spirit...let the *Ethnic Journal read...*
Many debts...and a lot of regrets...but~NOW...
Let's move on...and try to forget!!

The Scripture clearly denotes~~this report...
"Behold, I have given him...as a witness to the people,
A leader and commander~to the people...'
To rule in the midst of their enemies."

Now...Let us nurture and encourage...
This new environment...to become green and lush~
With the spirit of~Forgiveness...and Love.
These are moral values...of awareness~to increase...
Blending negative ones...into the harmony of peace.

Even Nebuchadnezzar~a biblical king of old...
Thought his 'God'...was gold...
Finally~~came to himself...and realized...
Only the most high God...had power over his life~
Who truly rules the heart...in the kingdom of men...
And complete authority to peruse~appoint~and choose...
Times...places and~ the end...Amen~

However~enlightened...by this knowledge...
His pride took a dip...from this folly...
So-he bowed down on his knees -~to pray...
'Lord help me please!' [interpretation:]
'Hey! I aint' all of that...no more than~
A big bag of cheese'.
The cold and callous mammal...playing the game...
Of Social Protection...competing for prosperity

And enjoying the fame...
Covering the world...like a wet red blanket...
Cloaked in White sheets of Christianity and...
Superiority...to justify innocent blood shed~
While in these disguises...Minorities are led!

But little did the demons know...
While screaming their epithets...and threats...
That the Lord's love and mercy...
Was a compensation for the bitter cup...of their 'Curses'.
He showed himself strong...in behalf of them~
Who loved him...while his power was revealed~
Through human weakness...the secrets were uncovered~
Of the evil wickedness.

Let's be alert...when the old Serpent grins~
With phony respect...at the colored tree leaves...
Pretending to be a concern...and loving friend!
Making them feel acceptable...like he did~
Adam and Eve...
Saying,~ "Just stay in your place...
and blow a cool breeze...
While we contaminate the flow...of political deeds!"

The ultimate goal...is to demolish the tree...
By pulling up the root...and its fertile seed.
But Almighty God~~is strong~
And his patience is long...
The tree will not be moved...
It is stamped~and~approved...
By the blood of Jesus~who forever rules.
Blacks are an essential part of that tree~~
Howling to be free...from the painful agony...

Patiently waiting...for their souls to be~reprieve...
When the Lord comes back~to retrieve.
He s that TREE...well fertile with the blood ~~
Of his Souls...
Who have been slain and martyred...
Filled with the 'Living Water'.

Multitudes~~drowned and beaten down...
Satan on the go~~rushing to and fro...
Seeking those...who are heavenly bound...
Because his ploy is~~to devour and destroy...
As he ask, *"What's up with you~~Boy?"*

I do beg your pardon~Sir,... "But my dreams~~
Are running over in my cup...
While I look up~to the hills...
From whence cometh my help...

And no weapon formed against me...shall prosper."

My help is in **Jesus**~who wept.
And He will come to separate...
The chaff from the wheat...for his name's sake...
And every tongue that rises~up...
Against the blood of the tree~~He will judge!
Because "in him...we live and breathe~
And have our being"...
As the "fighting is not against flesh and blood...
But against...Principalities~against Powers...
Against Rulers of darkness~Of this world...
And against Spiritual wickedness~~in high places."
He is coming back...with an outpouring~of his wrath...

He hath 'put down the mighty from their seats...
And exalted them of low degree'...
As He treads upon all evil...to receive his people!!
Surely~NOW...is "*The signs of the times*"...
For all to watch...and look up!
AMEN...AMEN...AMEN!!!

A BLESSED BIRTHDAY

GOD HAS BLESSED YOU...ALL OF THESE YEARS~
MOTHER DEWS...
AND YOU ARE STILL BEING USED~IN ALL OF HIS
SERVICES...
THAT HE SO CHOOSE...
HE HAS WATCHED YOU MANY YEARS~~GO THROUGH...
YOUR TRIALS AND TRIBULATIONS...
WITH A HEAVY HEART~~FULL OF TEARS...
BUT HE GUIDES YOU BY HIS HAND~~
IN EVERY SITUATION...SO THAT YOU ARE ABLE TO
STAND...
WHILE OBEYING HIS EVERY~COMMAND.

FOR YOU ARE PRECIOUS TO HIM...AND IN YOUR SPIRIT
HE PEERS...AS HE CALMS YOUR FEARS...AND...
MAKES LIFE'S STORM...CALM AND TRANQUIL

HE SAYS BE STILL...SO THAT HIS WHISPER CAN BE
HEARD...IN YOUR EARS...
BECAUSE HIS PRESENCE IS NEAR~~
FOR YOU TO FEEL...AND HEAR HIM SAY,
"BE OF GOOD CHEER, MY CHILD..."I AM ~ IS HERE!"

YOU ARE HIS SPECIAL CREATURE...THAT HE CREATED
AND PLACED...

INTO HIS SYMPHONY ~ OF SPIRITUAL HARMONY...
FOREVER PERMANENT~~IN HIS LOVING MEMORY.

HE SAYS...STAND STILL AND KNOW THAT 'HE IS'...;
OUR EYES...WHEN THEY BECOME DIM...

OUR MIND...WHEN OUR THOUGHTS ARE NOT
DEFINED...
OUR MOUTHS...TO CONDEMN THE WORDS...THAT'S
USED IN SATAN'S HOUSE...

OUR EARS...WHEN THEY BECOME DULL AND SILENT...
BUT CAN STILL HEAR HIS WORDS...THAT COME VERY
QUIETLY...

OUR HANDS...WHEN THEY START TO FOLD ~BECAUSE
TIMES HAVE TAKEN ITS TOLL...BUT IN HIS HANDS~HE
HOLD YOURS...TAKING AWAY THE STIGMA OF
"OLD"...SO THAT THEY BECOME NEW...
 OUR FEET...WHEN THEY REVERT TO BABY TODDLING...
HE STEADIES THEM...TO GO INTO THE RIGHT PATHS...
TO AVOID SATAN'S WRATH...

AND HE ASKS~~'HAVEN'T I ALWAYS BEEN THERE FOR
YOU?'
'DO YOU THINK THAT I BROUGHT YOU THIS FAR~~TO
LEAVE YOU...IN THE MURK AND MIRE OF ~ LIFE...?'
'YEA...EVEN WITH THE HOVERING OF SICKNESS~~WITH
THE STENCH OF DEATH...
WILL I NOT GIVE YOU NEEDED BREATH~~OF REST?'

MY SPIRIT GUIDES YOU...IN ALL OF MY WAYS...
BECAUSE ON THE CROSS...I WAS HUNG~~AND IN THE
GRAVE I WAS LAID~~TO SAVE AND REDEEM...

TO OPEN DOORS FOR YOU...THAT CANNOT BE SEEN...
AND TO REVEAL THINGS...THAT ARE SPIRITUALLY
~SUPREME.

NOW~YOU ARE COMING CLOSER...TO MY
OUTSTRETCHED ARMS...
LEAVING BEHIND ALL OF YOUR LIFE'S STORMS...
FROM A JOURNEY WELL DONE...TO RECEIVE A CROWN
WELL EARNED...

THEN FINALLY...MY WONDERFUL CHILD...
MY STORY...IN YOUR STORY...WILL BE TOLD!

SH-SH!!...NOW~STOP YOUR MOANING AND
GROANING...JUST GIVE ALL BURDENS TO ME TO
CARRY...I BEAR THEM FOR YOU~~GLADLY...

BECAUSE I AM~~BIG ENOUGH...STRONG ENOUGH...
POWERFUL ENOUGH...AND I AM EVERLASTING!!!...
AND THERE IS NOBODY...NOBODY !~ GREATER...
THAN I AM!!!

HUSH NOW! AS I WIPE AND DRY YOUR TEARS...*I AM*...
IS HERE! AND WILL BLOW MANY ~
BIRTHDAY KISSES...TO YOU...EACH AND EVERY YEAR!

EVANGELIST HENRIETTA DAVISON
COPYRIGHTED BY THE HOLY
GHOST
APRIL 6, 2013

THE BLESSED ONE

A day of magnificent grace...
God has bless you five scores and two years...and has given
you~ thirty -two
additional years...beyond
three scores and ten...which is the
promise

He has blessed you with mobility...
as the Holy Ghost guides~~your every footstep
Your spiritual and mental~agility have been blessed~~so that
you may worship him...
be an encouragement and inspiration ~~
to others...who feel they cannot travel any~~further

You are God's "Special Mark"...... liken to
Moses and his Ark~~as a guiding matriarch...
to be His covering~~for your family...friends...sisters and
brethren.

God has made you a strong fortress~
with doors that are blessed...
and when evil comes thru~~"No weapon formed against you
shall prosper" ~ and that's gospel!!

Your songs of praises and speaking the "Word"~~resounds,
with such intensity that the vibrations of the love of God~~is
clearly understood as they are~~heard.

The Angels sang and praised His Hold Name...Aunt Fannie...as
you were being born...on His Birthday and He graced this
earth with your presence~~for ONE HUNDRED AND TWO
YEARS...
You are a woman that's truly called~~the very essence of
"Blessings!"

© December 26, 2005
Henrietta Davison

I COUNT MY BLESSINGS/NEIGHBORS

I thank God for his many blessing and~favors
Here amongst my beautiful~Neighbors...
Whose caring and sharing are like rich
treasures buried in the rich earth~
of their hearts
And shared with undaunted~pleasures.

The tangible love from the community of
beautiful people...is a manifestation
of God's love~in all of his creatures...
as he illuminates in us...
the very essence~~ of his presence.

I thank you, Lord...for the Stegels~
Who has been here~~for me...
As my neighbors~~and my friends~
performing many deeds...
in a time of dire need.

Now, Lord...I ask you to breathe
your blessings~into their life and multiply.
Let each seed of love sown...
return one-hundred fold~strong!

And Lord...because of the Stegel's merciful deeds...
pour out special blessings~~
from your spiritual cornucopia~~
to fulfill all of their family needs...
And make me one of the good neighbors~~who
reciprocates like favors~~
In this scenic community of beautiful people~~
My Utopia!!

Henrietta Davison
© December 25, 2005

THE BLOOMING FLOWER

Nearly eighteen years ago...A seed was planted...
And germinated...in the core...
Of the Holy Ghost...
Then the roots began to spread...and take shape...
At the predestinated place...

The vine of admiration...was spiritually structured...
And irrigated...by lively discussions...
That entwined into a warm...and friendly relationship...
A blending of kindred spirits...blessed in heavenly bliss...

Thriving flower petals began to spring forth...and survive...
Blooming...flourishing and...becoming alive...on earth...
Nurtured by love...and Jesus' light...from above...

He approved and developed human unity...
With the persona of flowers...blossoming and blooming...
A smile...a light...a radiance of peace...and charity...
Sympathetic tears...shared in sadness...
Soothing words from the heart...note~letter...or a card...
Are souvenirs...from loving sparks...
To overshadow doom...and gloom...
And deliver our souls...from Satan's control...

Flowers intermingled...are complementary...
A quintessence of love...and humility
Blooming with the fragrance...of kinship...
Searching for God's...Holy touch...
As His petals...swirl from above...in a quite hush...

God chose a beautiful rose ... from one of His seeds...
Planted...long ago!
Known by the name of~Anita...to be a friend~Indeed!...
A plant~~a part of life...dispersed to help others in need...

A cheerful comforter...an encourager...an achiever
A true believer...in Jesus our Savior...and Deliverer...
A precious seed...a blooming flower...
That's chosen...from God's beautiful garden.

I thank God for putting *you* on my path...
My dear friend~my pal...
His shining light...is a constant reminder...
That keeps us humble in His sight...even when we stumble...
He is our Father...and we *are all* His children...
Thriving in His heavenly~~Flower Garden...
And the scepter of mercy is in His hand...to execute pardons...
And rescue us...from Satan's evil horrors...

We must always remember...*LOVE* is the key...*Jesus* uses...to
set us...**FREE!**
*TO "BE"...with **HIM** in all ETERNITY!* [eterni-te].....................

TO MY DEAR SISTER-FRIEND AND DAUGHTER
GOD LOVES YOU AND SO DO I!!!

HENRIETTA DAVISON, TRAVLING POETESS
Cpr August 12, 2014

A CALL TO ORDER...TO SERVE PASTOR, DARRYL & FIRST LADY, ANGELA BUSH

OH! WHAT A GREAT HONOR TO BE AMONG THE
WELL WISHERS FOR THE BELOVED PASTOR
DARRYL BUSH AND HIS LOVELY HELP-MATE~~
THE FIRST LADY...ANGELA BUSH...
AND TO BRING BLESSINGS TO GOD'S CHOSEN
RUNNERS, WHO ARE ON THE JOURNEY OF NEW
PATHS~OF AWARENESS...WHICH IS ANOTHER
LEVEL~OF SPIRITUAL MATURITY.

IT IS ANALOGOUS TO A BABY TAKING IT'S FIRST
STEPS OF UNSURETY...NEXT ~~ THE WALKING IS
TESTED FOR SURETY...AFTERWARDS ~~ THE
LITTLE FEET TAKE FLIGHT...RUNNING WITH ALL
OF ITS' MIGHT!

NOW...YOU WILL BE AWAKEN TO THE
DISCOVERY...THAT THE PAST WAS A MYTH OF
BLUNDERS AND WONDERS~~WHICH ONLY
ENHANCE THIS DAY AND TIME...WITH A
FRESHNESS AND NEWNESS~THAT IS SUBLIME.

HOWEVER, RAINSTORMS FULL OF THUNDER~~
WILL CONTINUE TO BE ON YOUR JOURNEY...
BUT YOUR EXPERIENCE EQUIPS YOU WITH
THE KNOWLEDGE OF GOD...TO RUN THROUGH
THE TROOP OF HARD KOCKS...AND JUMP OVER
THE WALL OF ROCKS~MADE LIKE A STRONG
TOWER...WHILE CONTINUING THE ASSIGNMENT...
MOVING IN THE HOLY GHOST POWER.

AND YOUR DIPLOMA OF SPIRITUAL VICTORY...
WILL BE YOUR REWARD ~ IN THE DUE COURSE
OF TIME...WHEN THE MYSTERY IS REVEALED...BY
THE HOLY SPIRIT...AND THE HOLY ROLE IS
SIGNED.

YOUR CALL TO ORDER~~OF DEDICATED
SERVICES~ARE DIRECTED AND BLESSED BY
FATHER GOD...
BECAUSE HE HAS HEARD THE MOANING AND
GROANINGS...AS HE LOOKED INTO YOUR HEART...

A CALL TO ORDER TO SERVE...WHILE FINGERS
POINT AT A WEARY~~AND BROKEN SPIRIT ``
BURDEN DOWN...WITH PERSECUTION AND LIES...
MEAN LOOKING FACES WITH ANGRY EYES...
WHILE LOOKING ALL AROUND...NOT A SMILE TO
BE FOUND!...

A CALL TO ORDER TO SERVE...WHEN YOU ARE
MADE TO FEEL UNWORTHY...WHILE THE
POSTURE OF UGLY BEHAVIOR~CONFRONTS YOU
UNLOVINGLY...

A CALL TO ORDER TO SERVE...WHEN RUN DOWN ON ONE SIDE BY YOUR SISTER...AND TORE UP ON THE OTHER~~BY YOUR BROTHER...WHICH CAUSES EMOTIONAL FORLORN...WHILE THEY POKE FUN!...

A CALL TO ORDER TO SERVE...WHEN YOUR DAYS ARE DARK AND DREARY...
AND YOU CAN'T SEE THE SUN THROUGH EYES~~ THAT ARE TEARY...

A CALL TO ORDER TO SERVE...TRYING TO MAX OUT TIME~THAT IS STEADILY DISAPPEARING... AS A RIGID SCHEDULE IS KEEPING YOU~TOO BUSY!!...

THE CALL TO ORDER TO SERVE... IS AT JESUS' FEET...A PLACE WHERE SATAN'S CLAWS~CAN NOT REACH...BECAUSE HE IS IN DEFEAT~~ WHILE YOUR SPIRITUAL ENERGY IS BEING STRENGHTEN...AND MADE FULLY COMPLETE!!

AND HE SAYS TO YOU IN ISAIAH 55:12...

"FOR YE SHALL GO OUT WITH JOY AND BE LED FORTH WITH PEACE; THE MOUNTAINS AND THE HILLS SHALL BREAK FORTH BEFORE THEE INTO SINGING AND ALL THE TREES OF THE FIELD SHALL CLAP THEIR HANDS."

I PRAY THAT GOD'S BLESSINGS WILL OVERFLOW
UPON YOU~~:
PASTOR DARRYL AND FIRST LADY BUSH.

EVANGELIST–HENRIETTA DAVISON, POETESS
MARCH 10, 2013

A CHOSEN LIFE

My dear Grandfather and Grandmother
Please do not fret~or have any regrets...
My short life on earth was chosen...
To be filled with laughter and excitement...
Like no other...forever!
No hands barred~and no paternal control...
Was my decision...to follow the mode...
Too late! I realized that it was the Devil's dare...
Who had led me there.

Forgive me for causing you~~ and my parents...this grief!
Since it was my choice...to follow Satan's lead...
Unforeseen...I had to pay the cost...

Pray and be of good cheer...his claws cannot reach me~here!
So dry your tears...my Grandfather and Grandmother...
Do counsel my sisters and brothers...and all others...
That their lives will not be sacrificed...for a quick fix of
An excited journey...by a false light of brightness!

At this time~~Grandfather and Grandmother...
A brand new life...has been discovered...
Be comforted that I am in a safe place...

So~please...release the burden of your heartache...
And weep no more...rather...pray...
That I will see God's face...when He carries me over~
To His heavenly Shore!

Henrietta Davison, Traveling Poetess
July 21, 2014

DEATH HAS NO HOLD
Dedicated To Cousin Virginia Fortè

The winds come and go...glowing to and fro...
No one can see it...but sounds are heard...
And the gust is felt...
So is death...in the quest for our breath...
Quickly~~he slithers in...souls are gobbled
And life is swallowed...
Then regurgitated into~the vastness of darkness.
We are never prepared to meet him...as he stealthily
moves...when suddenly our presence dissipates...
Our "Being" exudes...and merge into the heavenly state...
Where Jesus~~rules.

Death is just a fine line...or a whisper away...
And on the journey of time...there is~~no returning.
However, "Death has no sting and the Grave has no victory."
So says, the Holy scriptures.

We should stay ready...so that Jesus can receive...
And give us Spiritual credit...accordingly to our deeds...
If...only in Him~~we have believed.

Nevertheless, our mourning is heard...
And He sees our tears surge...like rivers of waters...
As we cry out~"Our Father"!
Wailing sounds like screeching music~

That rise to a crescendo...A sound of sorrow~
from a thudding heart...
A loss that has no similarity...an emotional tearing apart...a hurt that
has no comparison!

After the ocean waves~of suffering grief...

And the storm of rage~~subsides...
There is a quite whisper...at eventide
To let us know...the Holy Spirit~is by our side.
He is the calm~thru...and after the storm
Peace comes~~and healing~then...is performed.

Our father's love~gives us rest...
From the anguish of the loss...here on earth.
Family members and friends~~are blessed...
To return and be with Him...in a new birth...
Where there is no stress...and happiness~begins!

Yes~Death strikes covertly...
There is no certain time~~for his crime...
He swiftly strikes in families~~churches and countries,
At any given time.

However...The "Grim Reaper " ~is not our Keeper...
Because we belong to God our Father~~Our Savior Jesus~and the
Holy
Spirit~~
Who loves us...as their "Special People."
One day we'll be gathered~in their arms of power...
And they will comfort us...and bind forever...all of our weeping!

DEGREE'D

Traveling on unpleasant paths
My journey has brought me into an illuminated~~presence.
Deep valleys of problems...and
a tidal wave of sorrows...were passed...
And at last...conquering...all manners of defeat!~~
I press further...for higher degrees~
To be degree'd!

While~~I am moving towards another turning point~~
in my life...
The Lord is guiding me~as I run bear into a troop of warfare of
jealousy...hostility...and hate~that mock my fate.
Misuse and abuse~~conspiring to persecute~~and ensnare...
ready to swallow me up...if, in them~I entrust my care.
But~through it all...Jesus holds unto my hand...
While I leap over the walls of discouragement...
and utter despair.

Oh~h~how the tears...overflowed like a river...
from a quaking~and quivering heart...
But Jesus was there to lift me up...when the firey darts~~
of pain~~struck...
With Physical illness~Emotional insecurities...and Spiritual
scrutiny.

Seemingly, I heard Jesus say...I know your season is
humanly~unbearable...
but tenderly and lovingly...my hand will hold you~carefully.
Yes! I know the strife...of being a mother and a wife...
The exertion from the demands of a job...and your energies~~
robbed.
Yes! I heard your crying out...and your sobs!
So~~I will bless you...because you pressed~in me
And agreed...to be~~Degree'd!

Suddenly! The 'Light' was discovered...
That~thru my stumbling~fumbling and crumbling...
I was~already...in the radiance of Hope...
Because Jesus Christ~~is my spiritual support...
Manifested through the nurturing~~of the Holy Ghost!

Step by step...stone upon stone...I am~searching for an
appointment...with my destiny~~and purpose...on this path of
direction.
However...Satan tries to divert me...
pretending to be my friend...
Tempting me with a wilderness...of murk and mire~
Filled with sinking sands~of sin...
To drown me~~is his strong desire...
Because of God's calling on my life!~

Various degrees~~of enlighten'ment...and spiritual growth...
are ordered for my soul...
With Mercy and Kindness~~intertwined...
Even Love and Humility~are combined...
A special jewel~Jesus molds… to add to his eternal~scrolls.

My journey, sometimes...was traveled...in a valley of grief...
And a tide of suffering...
However...God held me high...above the rocky road...
And brought my mountains and hills low~~
Dried my tears and~~conquered my fears...
And by his love...the crooked paths that I chose~~were made
straight...and the rough road of hopeless'ness~
Were made smoothed...
Then my soul rested...and was not confused.

I agree to be Degree'd...as he spanks the puff of clouds...
to take me where ever I am sent...joyously~riding with a
smile...as the Holy Ghost carries me by his side.

Now...On my Academic Journey...I am blessed with a Doctorate
Degree...that only Jesus could help me...receive.
Therefore...I will move towards a different direction...
establishing fresh goals and objectives...
To enhance loyalty...harmony...and respect.

Behold...on this threshold of a new beginning...
I will encourage all ages...races and creeds to come together~~
in love...peace...and unity~~to savor the pursuit of
happiness...as we strive together~~for freedom.
Then...we may flow...into the nucleus of ecstasy~~with
exciting~fervor.

I will...now...look inside of me~~for Jesus Christ...
Who is my beacon of light~~
That beckons me...into his sight...
And I shall hear him say~with a voice
Like mighty winds~~in a hollow...
As a rush of many waters...

"MY CHILD...YOU HAVE BEEN FAITHFUL OVER A
FEW THINGS...I WILL MAKE THEE RULER OVER
MANY THINGS."

'I HAVE DEGREE'D YOU...
WITH A SPIRITUAL DEGREE!!

Congratulations~~Mrs. Eva Benson...on your high
achievement of your Doctoral Degree!

Henrietta Davison~Poetess
Copyrighted~~~May 8, 2009

DEDICATION TO PASTOR BUTLER & FIRST LADY~SISTER BUTLER

God called for the "Word"...to begin the creation~~eons...ago...
and when he spoke; The sun...moon...stars...plants and all kinds of
astronomical prodigies~~came forth...
Each being one of a kind...took their place~~in a unique design...
As he flung them all~~into outer space!
Then he molded and shaped every living creature from the ground...
animals...fowls in the air...various mammals~colossal, small and
round~~
making these species...rare~...
When the "Word" shouted...all sorts of weird Beings~~were called into
existence...~~Then...His creations~~were christened.
He blew upon them~~and there was no death in his breath!

After he had hung the earth~~in the Universe...
Later~~Man was created~~to commune with God~~attend the
gardens and
name the animals~~a facsimile of a family...
But God realized man was lonely...and rather than give him a
phone~~he put
the man to sleep...and took out a bone...
making him a mate that~~Adam called~~Wo!-man!...
[Interpreted~WOE
UNTO MAN!]

A helpmeet...to love~~and hold his hand...which was before~~the Big Deceit.

Millions of years later~~Milton Butler...was scooped up from the lead position in running school of gam'etes...and from the bank~of life... He was made~~complete... The slough of the birth canal...was the perfect slide...to enter into the world ~~in style Evenso in sheer terror...he howled.

But this did not compare to the haunting memory...of the flushing toilet bowl ... with him in it~~traumatizing his mind~~and soul. However~~this scene...was the Devil's~scheme... And at that very moment,...Satan put enmity between him~~and women... Causing wrath to be unleashed~~there was no peace... spewing out demonic venom...of bitterness and hostility... But the demons knew...that the day was coming~~when they'd be chased...and have to do some~~running.

Nevertheless, Satan proceeded to loose the~~alcoholic demon...thru his opening of distrust... Who jumped upon his back...and took him for his~~dastardly ride... right into the Church...before all of the fluttering and staring eyes... Like a proud equestrian~~~he sat astride...~

Ah Yes!! Since the beginning...the old serpent kicks up his ugly heels... To sneak upon~~to steal~kill...and destroy... So that we will have...very little joy...

...

My thoughts~~God ask, "Where have you been, Satan??"...I imagine
him
saying,...similarly, as years~ago..."Walking to and fro...upon all of the
earth to
find a special soul...name Milton Butler...who you, specifically,~chose...
So, that I may put hate and distrust in him~~
until his spiritual eyes~are dim."

And perhaps God said, "Why?"...and Satan says, "Just because~I...
can...
you know I am out...to destroy~~your man!"...

Much later~~the good Captain was appointed~~to the servant role...
on the
road to 'his' Damascus~~and then the Lord chose his running~~mate...
So, God prepared his helpmeet~~~Joan...to stand with him...thru the
storms~~
The perfect half~~he shaped...fitting her into the contours of his life~~
Complimenting each other~~as husband and wife

Subsequently...The good Shepherds opened a nursery...called the
"Little
Lambs"...and the "little scamps"...came from all over~~to hover...in the
beautiful meadow~~of love...
There were plenty of little sheep~~and a few little goats and rams~~for
the
Shepherds to keep...to be nourish with food and the "Word"...as unto
the
Lord~~they served...
As Jesus said, "Suffer little children and forbid them not, to come unto
me...for
of such is the kingdom of heaven."

Well~~the praying and nurturing...the good Shepherds
exhibited~~were heard all
over the City.

No matter how many times you both face...the demonic spirits
of~~Cain and
Rachel...
Just stay focus on your designated paths~~with servility and humility...
And break Satan's chain on souls~~who are bound up in his shafts.
Even when you are facing...familiar spirits~~like Cain and Rachel
Who were~~each...wroth with~~jealousy and hostility...
He...... because of rejected sacrifice~~and she...when her father
connived...
and made her sister...Jacob's first~~wife.

A woman...called to serve as First Lady...has few thanks and
small~~favors...
Her role has many facets...being the wife of her Pastor...
But being staunch and strong~~her patience is long...
as she quietly suffers~~many wrongs...
Of glassy stares and gnashing teeth~~breathing icy floes...
And the pelting of grievous words~~felt...could easily freeze...
the fires of~~hell.
So...on bending knees she is~~propelled...for Jesus is the only one to
tell~~about the wicked lying~~and evil conspiring...
causing her heartache and pain...making it difficult to abstain...from
retaliatory
actions~~that she sustains.

A wife covers her husband back as Abigail...discerned major danger...
hearing
that David was not~~without anger...

and rushed to stop a disaster...upon the household's Master...
She quickly took~~control...before David's rage could explode~~into a bloody
episode...
So, she brought him foodstuff...not knowing that it was in part~~her
dowry...for that unforeseeable~~hour...
and not the peace offering...for which she~~thought...but an act~~moving
her in destiny...to be David's~betroth.

Pastor Butler and First Lady Joan...you are together and not alone...
When called in order~~to serve...
While fingers point at the~~weary and broken spirits...
Burden down...with persecution and lies...mean looking faces with angry
eyes~~all around~~there are furrowed~~brows...

Making special dishes...would be a dream...if you didn't always have~~to clean
the kitchen!!
Not leaving much quality time for...listening~~at Jesus' feet...so that
spiritual energy can be replenished...and complete...
Remember Mary...who Jesus said, 'chose the good part'...
Even though Martha had a serving heart?

So at the helm of the ship...
You looked,...Pastor Butler,...at the Church~~as Paul had done...
knowing that a lot of things were in the future~~to learn...and
being full of fire~~you came in directly~
Rolling up your sleeves to explore the shores of "Good"...
Guiding this ship slowly~~but oh so boldly...you stood~~

Barking a loud decree..."We will not turn back! You'll see!"
And the trust of the crew~~was intent...cause they believed you were the
Captain~~sent...
To guide them with a holy hand...to God's great promised land...
And as you moved out~~into deep waters,
working with the crew became a bit~~harder.
But you continued...throwing out the spiritual~~raft...
Pulling in members from Satan's evil~~draft...
Pressing on with more force,...determined~~not to change your course...because you...
God had chosen~~!

And liken to the Man...who was walking through...exploring different environ
~~of lands...
Full of queries and filled with endless energies...gregarious~~with an assertive
persona...yet kind and compassionate...while searching for new frontiers...seeking new~horizons...
And making contemporary discoveries filled with many~~surprises...
Being analytical in his quest for knowledge~~while probing the spirituality of
life...

A Man...who fraternizes and mingles with all...whatever their status on the social
"totem pole"...
Carrying himself with the epitome of dignity and~~pride...
Captivating and convincing...but without the spirit to~~connive...
Speaking with quite authority~~appearing to be an open Book...
But wait! Take a second look!!

His depth cannot be measured~~or weighed.

Who is he~~that can effortless-ly guard his identity, feelings and
emotions~~from all who attempt to delve into the realm of his soul?
He commands respect as he appeals to the altruistic nature~of others.

A Man...seeking and walking in his destiny, while touching on the
lives of his
society...
Marching to God's drum beat~~with piety...
Exuding confidence...staking no claim that he is a Man...He Just Is!!

He stands tall and strong against life's adversities~~while walking
through
the valley of bitter atrocities...in the shadows of~~lurking death...
Handling all of his oppositions~~situations~with courage and...
determination...
As he Delivers the Word of God~~on life~living and~~love!

Pastor Milton Butler~~you are exemplary of that~~!God's Man!
And ever since that day~he called your name...your life transferred into
a spiritual
change...and from that time to this~~you have never been the same.
The battle for souls...is a continuation...and God is with you in every
situation.

Even, when the dark clouds~form...and you can't see in the~~storm...
There is no need to be alarm...for the Holy Ghost is in charge...
And you are directed by his arm!

© May 17, 2005
Poetess, Henrietta
Davison

THE PERFECT BIRTHDAY...ETERNALLY

As Jesus rose on the third day~~we were born.
O-oh!!~~what a glorious time for all of us~~when His resurrection
brought forth...a *special* shepherdess~~named **Joan.**
Thru her parents...she was birthed~~
To manifest His love~upon this earth.

Your journey was chosen...Yes!...and purposed
with Grace~~from above...
to monitor his flock~~and honor Him~the Rock!
And on each birthday that the Lord presents to you...
He maketh your path straight...to enter His gates~
Whereas...your heart is perfect...towards Him...
It is filled with good deeds...that you sow~~
like seeds in a gentle breeze~~they blow.

No matter how great the storms...or how loud the bell~gong
With gossip...deceit~and vicious lies~~
Just keep on singing your song...and don't be weary...
Because Jesus hears~~all of your cries!
And He *sees* every fiery dart!
Positioned here~~to break your heart.
Just stand still...you are fully equipped~~
With the Holy Ghost...who holds you lovingly~~
in His grip.
And you rose~~like the Phoenix...when He smashed into ashes the
scraps and traps~that was encountered...scattering them under your
feet~~to flounder.

Evenso...The years of tears~~will come...but must go...and be no more.
And the outpouring overflows...from high above~to the seashore of
'Love'...where Jesus stands...and reaches out his hands.

I hear Him say..."Come"...I have, now, ordained~~
your *earthly* birthday...and there will be others~for you~
To further attain.

But...these are merely shadows...of the
Eternal birthday celebration...where Angels will sing and dance...
with a glorious~stance~
Even...the very essence~~of His Holy presence...is radiant and bright...
Where gloom and doom...are transformed~~into light...

And at this particular time...Father God...Jesus~His Son...The Holy
Ghost~~and all the heavenly host...
Will engage in your celebration...of your Eternal birthday~
When you become~~"Ageless." And your Gift?...
Is Life...without strife........ For all Eternity!!

*Happy Birthday *~~*~~* Sister Joan Butler*
"The Traveling Poetess"
Henrietta Davison
March 23, 2008

© *March 14, 2008*

MY FATHER REMINDS ME OF HIS LOVE~~

ON YOUR JOURNEY OVER HILLS AND AROUND THE MOUNTAINS...YOU HAVE TRAVELED TO THE ETERNAL FOUNTAINS...TO DRINK OF GOD'S~~ BEAUTY~~MERCIES~~AND GRACE...

WHEN YOU LOOK ON HIS GLORIOUS FACE...BASKING IN HIS SHINY GLORY...YOU WILL NO LONGER FEEL THE PAIN~THAT WAS ENDURED...AS HE READS YOUR LIFE'S STORY...FOR HE HAS TAKEN YOU OFF OF THE PATH~OF STRUGGLING AND SUFFERING...
AND WHILE LOOKING AT YOU THERE~IN HIS HANDS...HE FILLS YOU WITH HIS LOVE...
WHERE YOU WILL NEVER~EVER~AGAIN...HAVE YOUR PEACE DISTURB!

HE IS SAYING~~I WAS WITH YOU THERE TO HELP YOU WITH YOUR CHILDREN...AS I USHERED THEM IN...
I STRENGHTEN YOU...
WHEN DOMESTIC ISSUES WERE TOO HARD TO BEAR...AND NO ONE~~REALLY~~SEEMED TO CARE...
I WAS THERE...
I WAS THERE...WHEN YOUR BURDENS FELT LIKE A HEAVY ROCK...

AND SOMETIMES~~YOU COULDN'T GET YOUR TEARS...
TO STOP...
AND I WOULD DRY YOUR EYES...AND LIFT THE
PRESSURE...BECAUSE YOU ARE MY SPECIAL TREASURE .

LO! I AM WITH YOU ALWAYS...UNTO THE VERY END...
AND ONE DAY...MY ANGELS...I WILL SEND...
TO BRING YOU TO ME...SO THAT YOU WILL BE ABLE TO
SEE...THE LOVE THAT I HAVE FOR YOU...AND IT WILL
FOREVER~~BE!

I HAVE PREPARED A PLACE FOR YOU TO BE WITH ME~
FOREVER~HERE IN HEAVEN.

YOU HAVE FINISH YOUR JOURNEY WELL~MY CHILD...
MY FAITHFUL SERVANT...

AND THE ANGELS AND SAINTS~I WILL TELL...
TO WELCOME YOU WITH SINGING...AND THE
CHIMING...OF HEAVENLY BELLS***

WORDS CAME TO ME FROM MY
FATHER GOD+++

THERE IS NO LOVE GREATER
FATHER GOD~LORD
JESUS~AND~HOLY GHOST
"A MESSAGE FROM MY FATHER"

THERE IS LOVE FOR YOU...THERE IS HOPE FOR YOU...
CAUSE I SEE YOU FROM ABOVE~
EVEN TO THE ENDS OF THE EARTH~
I SEND TO YOU...MY LOVE.

YOUR STRENGTH IS IN ME...
AND I CHASE YOUR ENEMIES~
FROM MY THRONE~THEM I SEE!
BECAUSE YOU ARE SO SPECIAL TO ME...

YOUR HEART IS FULL OF TROUBLES...
COME INTO MY ARMS~
AND BE CUDDLED...BECAUSE I LOVE YOU~SO!
WALK THROUGH MY DOOR...WHERE I AM AWAITING~
WITH OPEN ARMS...
THERE I WILL SING YOU SONGS...
TO HELP YOU THROUGH THE STORMS.

I WILL GIVE YOU REST...
AFTER YOU TAKE THE TEST

TO ASSURE YOU THAT I AM THERE...
AND DO KNOW WHAT IS BEST!

I HEAR YOUR EVERY PRAYER...
AND HAVE CHOSEN YOU~TO BE CHOSEN...
I WILL HOLD YOU CLOSE~TO MY HEART...
WHERE YOU ARE...
AND I AM EVERYWHERE...I LOVE YOU SO!...
YOU ARE MY Soul!

Evangelist, the traveling poet-
ess ~ Henrietta Davison

MY FRIEND...MY SECOND SKIN
Dedicated to my Sister Friend and Second Skin..."Claudi'-Ma"

MY FRIEND~~MY SKIN...WHERE DID IT ALL BEGIN?
WAS IT YESTERDAY~~OR A DECADE
WHEN OUR RELATIONSHIP WAS MADE...
BY OUR HEAVENLY FATHER...?
YES...HE WAS...THE ALMIGHTY AUTHOR!

HOWEVER, THE BEGINNING WAS TURBURLENT AND
OUTRAGEOUS...
EVEN NOW...SOME THINK WE ARE CRAZY
NEVERTHELESS...IT IS TRULY AMAZING!
HOW~~GOD CAN TURN THE WORLD~~UPSIDE
DOWN...AND TURN HIS SOULS COMPLETELY~AROUND...
WHEN THERE IS NO SOLACE...OTHERWISE~TO BE
FOUND.

LISTED IN SCRIPTURE HISTORY...WAS A DAUGHTER
NAMED RUTH...WHO REFUSED TO TURN...FROM HER
MOTHER-IN-LAW~NAOMI...
FOR THERE WAS NO DESIRE...TO BECOME A LONELY...
ROAMER...
SINCE HER KIN...WAS LIKE A SECOND SKIN.
LATER...FINDING FAVOR~AS ANCESTRESS...
TO OUR SAVIOR.

THEN THERE WAS JACOB'S WIVES...
LEAH AND RACHEL...SISTERS IN RIVALRY~
FOR THE LOVE OF JACOB...
GIVING THEIR HANDMAIDS...TO SURROGATE~
AS SECOND SKINS...
SO THE SISTERS COULD COMPETE...
AND CLAIM THE PARENT ROLE~OF KIN.

SOMETIMES~~WE LOOK AROUND...
TO CONFIDE IN A FRIEND...
ABOUT THE STRUGGLES AND STRIFES...
SEEMINGLY...THERE IS NO END...
BUT WHO CAN FEEL THE CRISIS~OF LIFE...
THE HURT AND PAIN...WHILE TEARS ARE FALLING...
LIKE DROPS OF RAIN?
ONLY A FRIEND~WHO IS AKIN...
TO A SECOND SKIN!
HOWEVER~~EACH ONE OF US HAS THE NEED...
TO SHARE~DISCUSS~AND INTERCEDE...
WHEN THE DOORS OF MERCY CLOSE...
AND OUR FAMILY DECIDES TO OSTRACIZE...
NEVERTHELESS...WE ARE NOT TO AGONIZE...
BECAUSE THE HOLY GHOST...IS ALWAYS NIGH...
TO MAKE US SPIRITUALLY~KIN...
SO THAT ON EACH OTHER~~WE CAN DEPEND...
WHILE HE FIGHTS OUR BATTLES...TO DEFEND~AND
WIN!
WE ARE INDEED...SISTERS...FRIENDS~~AND SECOND
SKINS!

THEN THERE WAS JOHNATHAN AND DAVID...

CLOSER THAN BROTHERS...
AND BEING PROTECTED FROM SAUL...
DAVID'S LIFE WAS SAVED...
AND IN THIS ONE PARTICULAR THING...SAUL'S
SON...DISOBEYED...
BECAUSE HE LOVED DAVID MORE~~
THEN JUST A FRIEND...HE WAS LIKE A SECOND SKIN!

I THANK GOD OUR FATHER~AND THE LORD JESUS...
AND HOLY GHOST...FOR THE BOND OF
FRIENDSHIP...LOVE...PEACE...RESPECT...AND THE
SINCERE CARING...ABOUT ONE ANOTHER'S
FEELINGS...THAT IS HARMONIOUS WITH A SPIRITUAL
KINSHIP...
THAT IS CLOSE...AS A SECOND SKIN+++

HENRIETTA DAVISON...POETESS
"CPR' MAY 10, 2013

GOD'S STEPLADDER IN PLACE

GLORY TO GOD… who honors whom ever~he chooses…
To perform in special services…for his purposes…
So that his light beams…on those that are redeemed…
And follow not~Satan's schemes…

But hearts sealed with Jesus love…is respected and protected~
With successful blessings…
And by anointed appointments…his people are empowered…
Via God's healing waters…
Drawing others to the well…of spiritual health…
Where his powerful presence…is felt!

Jesus says "Come my child…walk in my light…
There is no darkness in me…
The sun shines thru my sight…
And the moon beams in the direction…
of my reflection!

'You are called by my decision…to a new position…
A woman unique…ornamented…and a marvel…
While being addressed…as Chief Master Sergeant…
An assignment that causes…'kicking up dust'~'making a fuss'…
And 'Spewing out words of curses'!
But be not dismayed…it's only the devil's ways~of illogic!'

However...a woman called to serve...not only gives life
But preserves life~with her life!
Yea! There is a high price to pay...with tears that flow...
Down by the river of Jordan...on the stormy seashore.
Evenso...Women continue to be on a mission...
Submitting to atrocious...and turbulent conditions.

Howbeit!...God's mystery...in this role particularly...
Is the acceptance of the scepter...of mercy...
To assist hurting souls...
And to exert the authority...that he commands...
For He holds ALL of his children~of ALL colors...
In the palm of His hands...
And no matter what the circumstances are...
Following in the footsteps of Jesus...
Is the highest degree~of authority.
He is the Almighty Director...of his creatures...
And demands respect...for his choices!
After all...He is the BOSS~of bosses!

There have been significant contributions...
Made by Black American women
Some...who~sacrificed their lives...for better living conditions.
To name a few~that are Historically listed~are:

Barbara Jordan~the first black woman elected to the Texas
Senate...As a United States Representative...
Spearheading laws to bring equality to all...

Selma Burke~a Sculptor...was selected over twelve other artists~
to create a bronze bust of President Roosevelt, who sat for two

days instead of the two hours allocated. It was replicated on the dime...and today the bronze bust is displayed...in the Recorder of Deeds Office~in Washington, D.C.

Mary McLeod Bethune...was the founder of Bethune Cookman College...using one dollar and fifty cents... To open her first school...

Harriet Tubman~an abolitionist...became the "Conductor" of the Underground Railroad... Bringing slaves to freedom...Despite her blackouts... An injury that came about...At the age of thirteen... A rock thrown by her master...caused this disaster! Nevertheless~~Jesus redeemed~and used her to glean... She had no doubt...of being a leader...as His Reaper... Sometimes called..."Moses of her people"!

At this time...we have~~Michelle Obama~as being the First Black American~~First Lady...Of the United States of America... Eyebrows are being raised...across the nation...with smiles faked and in place... Because of her advocacy for the wellness of children...promoting an agenda...for healthy and nutritious food...in schools... A cause defended...to help all children... By our Father~"Who art in Heaven"...all families are kindred!

Dr. Maya Angelou...a famous poetess...who brought attention... To an oppressed and downtrodden people~~ Thru her poetic expression...leaving a legacy of Hope...as she look beyond blight an despair...from the scope of the rope...sharing her enlightenment of true life...which she found within... Revealing the background of the journey of struggles...

From the beginning~as a child...who rose above~~
the cruelty...and ugliness...
To be an inspiration to others...who are suffering from the crashes
and whacking~~of life.
And despite the encounters of strife...
God helped her to climb...the rugged ladder of battles...
And with a smile...she is now saying...But, "YET I ARRIVED!"

These...and thousands of other outstanding...souls

As our History unfolds...refuse 'Big Foot's' evil demands...
'To stay in their place'! A death and doom phraseology...
Where a future of darkness looms!!

And now!!...Regina C. Buckhalter...
You have been selected...empowered...and promoted...
As Chief Master Sergeant...
of the United States Air Force...
And called to order...for the position...as a chosen vessel...
In God's court...
To be a living testimony...standing before His alter...
Sharing His Word as a healing balm...
To inspire downtrodden~souls...
And to administer mercy...to those in your control...
While creating a circle of love...that cannot be disturbed.
Let it ignite sparks of joy~peace...and harmony...
To reflect His light in the enormity...of the Universe!!

Your future holds mighty works...to be performed...
Be ye armed...and spiritually calm...
And just lift up your feet...you are not in defeat...
God's stepladder is in place...the race is already won!

He will not let you~falter...
CHIEF MASTER SERGEANT REGINA C. BUCKHALTER!
Because **there is no beginning~nor ending...of love~for**
you...that's Pouring from the heart of the "LIVING WATERS"
and **the** "ROCKS OF GIBRALTAR!"
These inspired blessings are encouraged by Father God~Lord Jesus
And Holy Ghost!

Evangelist~~Henrietta Davison,
Traveling Poetess
Cpr. May 21, 2014

JESS:

I pray that the sparkling lights~that shines...
So bright~from within your home~
Will shimmer over the waves of gushing waters~~
Enhanced by the warmth of family laughter...
That calms the angry storms of life...with kindness~~
Love~and peace~~
Which flows amidst mankind~~
Farther than the eyes can see.

Your quiet strength of mercy and compassion...
Are felt by all that you encompass...
And is liken to the soft humming of trees...
Making cosmic sounds~~by singing leaves...
Crooning tunes...and dancing blooms.

Your caring and peaceful spirit is truly...
a Blessing...to all who are under undo~stresses.
You are...the quiet still waters~~ordained by God~~
Our Holy Father!

Poetess, Henrietta Davison
Copyrighted, February 8, 2011

THE BEGINNING OF HEALING

As the moans **and** groans are heard from the roof~~
Let them be sounds of uttered...proof~
That our God is merciful and is the Almighty of~truth...
Let the manifestation of each cry be a resounding memory~that
He is the "Living Balm" releasing the healing...of all the years
of physical pain~and emotional strain.

Let the healing begin in our children~~and their
children...breaking generational curses of...
hate~hostility~unforgiveness~~jealousy~
Lying~backbiting~resentment~and discontentment.
These demons literally,~destroy us...and others.
THIS SHALL STOP AND GO NO FURTHER!!
As we bind them in a sheaf that's tight~holding on to Jesus
~~with all our might ...While preparing for the spiritual~fight.

Let the healing begin~from every sound and groan...of the soul...
That diminishes all anger, animosity and all demonic atrocities
... manifested from generation~to generation.
These are bound and cast out~from our families~~now!
To instill the sweet savor love~peace...and harmony.

Let the healing begin from this day forward...
Not looking back into the pits of~~darkness...
And the bitterness that it brought.
We will now...march to the drum beat of a new beginning...

walking in the light of love...which comes from Father God~
above...
Forgiving and being forgiven...willing to be servants...ready to
serve~~without grudges.

Let the healing begin...when the skin tightens~~clinging to the
bones...
Which refuses to be filled with flesh...
And the grim thoughts of "I am all ~ alone" ~~
are enmeshed in helplessness...

Let the healing begin as children turn...
toward each other~in a circle of love...
Which no longer disturbs~ and
The darkness of the past...cannot last and is forever lost...into
yesteryears' journey...
As we look to a bright future...with yearning.

Nevertheless...
Jesus has blessed you, Donnie...as you are now resting in the
sweet bliss of happiness...encircled by Jesus' arms...surrounded
by his Angels~at the eternal heavenly~throne.

Satan...our souls~~you cannot steal
We will move forward to be healed~~
Our mouths are filled with praise~~with voices
raised .. in melodious humming...of love~peace and
spiritual harmony~~

Now~I cry ~BOLDLY "O' Death~where is your sting?
O' Grave where is your victory!

Poetess Henrietta Davison
Copyrighted September 18, 2009

A NEW JOURNEY

Another crossroad on your journey...
Leaving behind family~friends~Church...
And even some enemies...

Nevertheless...time moves on...
And so do we...
But what! You are taking a part of our hearts...
Evenso...you are leaving a great portion of yours.
After forty years or more...
How can the tears not gush~~as it flows?
Not penetrate our very souls?
While we are engrossed in...how much~~
You will be missed.

Ah 'h- Yes...'The how are you felling today'?...
Telephone calls...or the dropping by
To see if we are~OK...
Or 'I thought this little gift looked like you'...
These are only a few things...that you do.
All for~FREE!

Money cannot buy...the beautiful attitude~
Nor smiles...that you both bestow...
Upon souls~who are in need.
Yes...we will miss you~indeed!

The neighborhood is filled with testimonies...
That would take a book...to fully~review.
For instance~~climbing a flight
Of stairs~right after heart surgery...
To carry food that was prepared...
And to encourage~
An elderly member of the Church
Because both of you cared...

No big deal~~Did I hear someone say?
But right after heart surgery?
I believe that Jesus...accepted her sacrifice...
As a sweet savor~of love and caring...
While the sister was caught up in the expectation~
Of taste!

The reaching out and sharing your home to...
Homeless souls~
I further believe...has earned precious stones...
In your impending...Crown~~of Gold...
From our Father...Lord Jesus...and the Holy Ghost!!!

My Dear Brother and Sister...
We the Church are in deep prayer...
Because~there has not been enough time...
To prepare~
A replacement...of many~Years...
Consistently...with meticulous care.

Who can come to the rescue~in a split second...
To stop the rain from running over the pews...
Who can keep the electricity in peak condition...And...
Who will keep the plumbinga going in the kitchen.

Will the coffee pot~paper plates~cups...
And other wares...be in its proper place?...
Remember~nothing can be out of order there!

Oh~!h! How We Will Miss You!
Precious "SERVING SERVANTS" ~ of The Lord!"
Nevertheless...you have well served...your time...
On this path~~Of your Journey.
You are leaving a path filled with love...
But Jesus has another path that's overflowing...
With His Love and Blessing~~

And we feel that you have proven yourselves
Worthy and most certainly...DESERVING!!!

With Heart Felt Love,
Henrietta Davison, the Traveling Poetess
December 31, 2011

THE LIVE DOLL

Rag dolls were prevalent in...
Black families...
Deep in the woods~of the back country...
In little run down shanties...
Hidden behind big white houses~for miles...
That concealed the squalor~in the hollow...
Of mandated Lifestyles.

Stuffed stockings were used~
As the body...for a doll...
Rags and sometimes~ears of corn...
With its silken strings for hair...
Which helped~to form the head...
The other was for body...to be homemade.
Hence...a 'play baby'~was born...
To share feelings of~care...and despair.

Not so with our white playmates...
Who had beautiful dolls~in their image...
Long straight hair...beautiful eyes~~
With long lashes~
After their fashion.

Finally...in times...BuckWheat~~
Was created...

With rolling eyes~and kinky hair~~
That shaped his face...
And a wide smile...showing big white teeth...
To make him complete...
Not a toy...for the black kids~to enjoy...
But to make mockery of them...to tease...
Was the ploy!

Finally...the day came...and nothing...
Has ever been the same...
Since~God blessed me...with a beautiful doll...
A charismatic and loving child...
With a sweet smile~that was royal
Interacting happily~with everyone...
She was so much fun.
Even strangers~drew nigh...and didn't want
To say good-bye.

The barrier was~also...broken...
When I brought my doll~to school...
Which was not a policy~~nor general rule.
But teachers and students~loved her...
And thought it was so cool!!

My doll grew up to be a fine and...
Lovely young lady.
A countenance of compassion~
And a caring heart~for others...
Which drew many to her...including
Her brother~~
Even...when she swung out of order...
To discover life and be~
Worldly-wise...

Which caused daughter...to turn into motherhood...
Removing the doll position~for good...
Nevertheless~God kept her in his hand...
Abating~~Satan's destructive plan.

A special gift...was given to her~by Jesus...
How to interact with kindness...and meekness...

An understanding heart...a sense of humor...and...
In depth spiritual discernment...
To share with others~~while on her journey.

Yes...I thank Our Father God...Our Savior and Our
Holy Ghost!...
Bringing her out of the "Bowels of Hell"
While teaching her that Jesus is Real...
And the Holy Spirit...is "Truth"...
And that Father God guides us...in his Son Jesus...by
The quickening of the Holy Spirit...
And...just for a short time~~Satan is only temporarily~~
Running wild...like a 'Loose~Goose'!

I thank them for letting my real "Doll"~~ hear it...
Rebirthing her into a life of Godliness~~
By Spiritual anointing...of his "Holy Oil"!

Love you!! ~~~~Your Mother,
Henrietta Davison, the Traveling Poetess
January 3, 2013

SISTER~SISTER...MY FRIEND~~
ETHEL BIVINS

Many rushing winds~of life's vicious storms...
Brought tidal waves~of sorrow and fear...
That punched and suppressed sisters...
Through years~of daily tears.

We are women created by God...
Made in a special way...right from the start...
With similar heart beat of love...
Sensitive to the needs...of each other~
Without concerns for~skin color.

Howbeit!...the transparency of our souls...
Is what blend us...
The flow of tears...the cheerfulness that shows...
The smile that glows...clouds of sadness...
Lurking misfortunes...and madness...
All are emotions...carried on the threshold...of fate.
Come!...we are just a sister~away!

Come let us comfort one another...
Pick up the phone~so that our needs can be known...
A letter...a look...a soulful moan...after being scorn...
Is a time to reach out to one another...with a heart forlorn...

A sympathetic expression...that makes us strong...
Which eliminates the need...to suffer alone.

Jesus has decreed...these faithful words~indeed...
That all souls are his...and he further conveys...
That we are his children...brothers and sisters...
Just a sister~away!

The "Traveling Poetess," Henrietta Davison
Copyrighted...March 19, 2012

A SUFFEERING SERVANT

Bishop Rowe~a blessed woman~~eventho put to the test...
Of losses from diverse~~causes...
Loss of family members~in death...
Loss of homes...loss of health~~and some wealth...
God was there~to give you rest.

He has called you to serve~~by the power of his love...
Even with the 'thorn' in your side~like Paul~~
You may slip and slide...but not utterly fall~
Cause He holds you in his arms~~through it all.

For to suffer...represents Jesus' walk on earth~~that's in
the Word.

He was pierced in his skin~
"Bruised for our iniquities"...and carried to the Cross~
The world's sins~~
So that Father God could be glorified~~in the end.

Yes...Bishop Camellia and Pastor Amos Rowe...
God has called you both...into his court...
And chose you...to help reap the harvest~of lost souls...
Where workers are few...and the labor is grievous...

And to motivate those souls~languishing in the pews~
Working their mouths...only calling the name~Je~sus...

Your call to order...of dedicated services...is directed and

Blessed by the Spirit of Father God...
He knew your desire to work...and...
Chose an integral part...close to his heart!!

With every nail that was hammered...
As a carpenter in your trade~Pastor Amos Rowe...
Your prayers resonated...like
the trumpet of Joshua...in the battle of Jericho.
Your spiritual request~~has been addressed...to be a
handyman for Jesus...
To help souls stand...

And follow the true Carpenter's commands...
Whose building was not made~by hands.
Jesus tightly fitted and framed...a new order~

Here on earth...
Assembled and bonded...fashioned and transformed~
So that the Spirit Man born...
Would be the reflection of Him...Nailed~~to the Limb.

Courageously...standing by your wife~~you share your
life...being faithful with prayer and supplication...as she
faces trials...and tribulations~
Health challenges...which are constant battles.
You are, indeed...a beacon of caring light~
that shines on her suffering~of agony and pain...
Unwavering under pressure~being slow to complain.

Your love is expressed through concerns...compassion and
patience...
Surely...Jesus is the reason~~
That you are true...and hold, firmly, to her hand.

Yea! Pastor...and Bishop you are in a mighty fight...
But 'the battle is mine saith the Lord...continue to abide~
While he wields the Rod~~with his might!
He never loses...keep him in your sight!

Camellia Rowe...you unfold like the strong shiny leaves and
Various colors...of the Camellia flower...
You thrive not only in warm regions~~but in all seasons~
Of life
Challenges are confronted...and awkward trials~are
Overcome.

Evenso~~Your ministry journey of twenty-five years...have not
been without storm~rain...and many tears...
Indeed~some battle fronts...have been faced with fears...
Nevertheless~~multi talents were unfold...
Music~teaching...preaching and different languages
Speaking...and other success stories can be told.

As its founder and builder~~the "Glorious Praise Christian
Fellowship Ministry"...came in existence...
Subsequently...CJ Rowe Christian Academy, also, became a
school of merit...for young people.

Your astuteness as a visionary...
Saw the need~to bring into fruition...

The HEROWES Program..."Home Education Reaching Out With Excellent Systems..."
And was established...due to your heroic~~persistence.

Now you have been appointed and anointed for another assignment...Bishop Camellia Rowe and Pastor Amos Rowe... Ministries...
Ordained and proclaimed by Father God~~who looks not on personal attainments...but seeks love in the~heart.

A Call to order~To Serve...is not without suffering...but a call and command for obedience.

A Call or order~To Serve...when fingers point at your weary and broken spirit~~!with persecution and lies...emphasize with furrowed brows...and mean looking eyes...

A Call to order~To Serve...when you are made to feel ~unworthy~~while trying to be loving...

A Call to order~To Serve...being talked about...run down on one side by your sisters...and tore up from the floor up...by your brothers...

A Call to order~To Serve...when your days are dark and dreary...and you cannot see the sun through eyes~~that are teary.

Bishop Camellia Rowe and Pastor Amos Rose~your Installation and Ordination in the Kingdom Builders Missionary Ministries: Is your Call to order~To Serve...By installing and teaching your parishioners Jesus' first commandment...that they love God with all of their hearts, mind, and soul...
and second to this is: Love thy neighbor as thyself.

A Call to order~To Serve...To Impart your love!
With guidance and patience~~worship and praises...
Nurturing with kindness and mercy~to all who hunger and
Thirst after righteousness...

A Call to order~To Serve...To Invest time in leadership
building...and sending competent leaders out...to harvest the
field of plenty.
Bishop Camellia Rowe and Pastor Amos Rowe...The Spiritual
Baton of a "Suffering Servant" is passed on to you.
As you travel on your journey~there is no looking back...nor
returning...you must keep running.
For Jesus said, "No man having put his hand to the plow, and
looking back, is fit for the kingdom of God."

Remember...!! The Comforter~who is the Holy Ghost...will
Lead and guide you...to the reward...which is great and
Everlasting...if you endure to the end...

Remember...! In the very beginning ..
Father God...presented his son, Jesus...
As a "Suffering Servant"
and a living sacrifice...shedding his blood...
to cover our sins...
So that we could be renewed...
And our souls could be saved...
All because of his Love!

SLOW DOWN CHARIOT!

Now~~my flaming Chariot...take me beyond the
Boundary~~of the physical...and into the present Being~~
Of transparency...
Where...the questions are answered~
As they manifest...continually~~the Blessings of eternal life.
And the power of our Father's love...reveals the Spiritual
Realm...
When we choose to abide~in him.

Swing down Chariot...Don't waver in the sky...
Deliver my spirit to my Father God...
There...in him~~I will abide~~
As a work of art~~scrolled in his heart~
Made of clay...I must obey...I cannot stay!
Close the door~~Satan...! You cannot wreak havoc~~
In my life...Anymore!

Swing low~w...Chariot! And take me home...I have been
here suffering~~much too long...
Let the moaning and groaning~~be gone...
I am ready to sing a new song~~
"Of Eternal life...heavenly living...and a new beginning."

Swing down Chariot...and let me ride into the skies~~Leaving all of
my sickness and heartaches and pain...

They will fall from me...when I snatch them off...
Like~~snow flakes...and drops of rain...
Similar~to Elijah's mantle~~caught in Elisha's hand.
Whoa Chariot! Stop and pick me up! Take me away~
Beyond the trees...
So my soul will be appeased!!
Now...I must go to my Father~~
Where Satan...cannot follow!

WAVES OF SORROW

Riding the waves of sorrow...
Behind the doors of gloom~~that hides in the shadows...
While enclosing the future~~as it unfolds...
To cover that is soon...coming ashore.

We travel through the wilderness...
Of the horrors of~darkness...
Which strives to cover the brightness...
That will shine on our tomorrows...

O'oh! Lord! Let me walk carefully...in quietness...
To enjoy~NOW~~the essence of your presence
Blow your breath...into me~with your
Holy Caressing.

Oh let me enjoy the moment~~that I can find...
Even when the Sun does not shine...
When Euroclydon rushes in...being not sublime...
To blast us into...the signs of time

Let me rise up from between...Scylla and Charydis
Giving praises to our Father...our Savior~the Living
Water...
And to the Holy Ghost~who brings us through...

Help me trust in the Holy Three~~who is each one of
YOU!
OH~GOD!...My father...I was blessed to enter~
This world...riding a canoe...of water in blood
And when I slipped from side to side...to one path~then
another...
You were there to guide~~and direct me further...

With love and patience~you were there beside me...
To hear my prayers...and then to save me...
And take me on...another journey...
Where there are no clocks with time~
Minutes nor hours...
But gardens of blue...and purple flowers...
And the heavens glow~with streets of gold...
Being encircled...by a radiant rainbow...
Which glitter...and sparkle...while beauty unfolds!

HAPPY FATHER'S DAY

D~~Daddy...to youths, searching for a leader with integrity...

W~~Worker...helping others who are in need ..

A~~Always...ready to learn new things...

I~~Inquisitive...about God and spirituality...

N~~Nice and kind to others...

E~~Energetic...with love for life...

G~~Garden .. fresh with flowers of love for all!!!

May the love of GOD~His Holy Son JESUS and HOLY GHOST
COVER YOU ALL THE DAYS OF YOUR LIFE~
WITH BLESSINGS!!!

HAPPY FATHERS DAY!!!

LOVE YOU~Moms Dear

FUNNY!~~FUNNY! WHAT'S FUNNY? AM I FUNNY? FUNNY! FUNN~~Y! WHAT'S FUNNY?

SISTER CLEMMIE CALLED ME LAST WEEK AND WAS TELLING ME ABOUT THE WOMEN'S DAY PROGRAM THAT SHE WAS PLANNING AND SHE WAS CALLING IT A "SALAD/TEA"...AND I THOUGH, "HOW UNUSUAL!" ~ "SALAD/TEA...WHAT'S THAT? I ASKED. SO, SHE WENT ON TO FILL ME IN ON THE DETAILS AND ALSO THAT FACT THAT SHE WANTED THIS TO BE FUN~~AND COULD I THINK OF SOMETHING FUN. "FUN?"...I SAID "WHAT KIND OF FUN THINGS?"
"YOU KNOW FUNNY...SOMETHING FUN!", SHE REPLIED. I TOLD HER I WOULD TRY TO COME UP WITH SOMETHING.

I THOUGHT AND THOUGHT...I COULDN'T THINK OF ANY FUN GAMES...I HAD TOLD HER ABOUT SOME KIND OF GUESSING GAME...AND SHE ASKED, "WILL THAT BE FUN...A LITTLE SKIT, MAYBE?"
"I DUNNO, LET ME THINK AND GET BACK TO YOU." I THOUGHT, "SKIT? WHAT KIND OF GAME SKIT?...I MUST BE **WAY** BEHIND THE TIMES!!"
I COULD JUST SEE EVERY ONE ELSE PLAYING THESE LITTLE FUN GAMES...AND I CONCLUDED

THAT I WOULD PARTICIPATE...RATHER THAN BE
A PRESENTER...I'D JUST TAKE PLEASURE IN WHAT
OTHERS PRESENTED...I NEVER WAS ANY GOOD AT
INITIATING SOCIAL GAMES, HOWEVER, I DID ENJOY
THEM.
BUT THEN I REMEMBERED THE BABY SHOWER THAT
I HAD RECENTLY GONE TO AND ONE OF THE GAMES
WAS PUTTING BEADS AROUND EVERYBODY'S NECK
AND WHOEVER HEARD THE PERSON WEARING
THE BEADS...SAY THE FORBIDDEN 'WORD' ~~~ WAS
ENTITLED TO TAKE THE BEADS OFF OF THAT PERSON'S
NECK. THEN, I THOUGHT ... NUN-UNH!! THAT WILL
NEVER WORK WITH A SISTER...TAKING BEADS OVER
HER 'LAID BACK-DO'...**OR HAT**...I THOUGH ABOUT
MINE! I SURE WOLDN'T FANCY SOMEONE DRAGGING
BEADS OVER MY HEAD~~PULLING OFF MY HAT! THE
LORD KNOWS WHAT YOU WOULD SEE UNDERNEATH...
AFTER A PRIVATE SUMMER EPISODE!! BUT IT WAS OKAY
FOR OUR OTHER SOFT HAIRED SISTERS...CAUSE THEY
COULD SHAKE THEIR HEAD AND THE HAIR WOULD
FALL BACK IN PLACE...BUT THAT DOESN'T WORK FOR
US ~~**SUSTERS**!! HA! YOU MAY REACH OUT A HAND
AND
DRAW BACK A 'KNUB'...! NO, I'D BETTER LET THIS IDEA
DIE
...RATHER THAN A BODY!
NO, CAN'T MESS WITH THE 'FRO'...THIS NOTION HAVE
TO GO!

LATER ON, I TOLD SISTER CLEMMIE THAT I JUST
COULDN'T THINK OF ANYTHING TO PRESENT THAT
WAS FUN...MIND YOU, I AM THINKING
ABOUT GAMES...

UNTIL SHE ASK, "DON'T YOU HAVE SOME POEMS–THAT YOU CAN DO, THAT'S FUNNY?" I SAID, "WELL-L, MAYBE SARAH." OH-OH! I HAD TO REVERSE MY THINKING ABOUT ENJOYING SOMEONE ELSE'S PRESENTATION~~SHE MEANS FOR ME TO PERFORM!!... **ME**??? THEN SHE ASKED, "HOW MANY DO YOU THINK YOU CAN DO? TWO OR THREE, MAYBE, BUT YOU KNOW **SOMETHING LIGHT...SOMETHING THAT'S FUN...YOU KNOW...FUNNY**?...CAUSE YOU KNOW, GIRL, YOU DO SOME HEAVY STUFF!" I SAID, "UNHUNH..., YEAH...KIND OF." FINALLY, IT DAWNED ON ME~~SHE IS TALKING ABOUT A **PROGRAM...BIG TIME**!!!

I ASKED, "IS THERE ANY ONE ELSE ON PROGRAM?"... SHE SAID, "WELL, I THOUGHT **YOU COULD CARRY IT~~SOMETHING FUNNY.**" I SAID, THIS IS SUCH A SHORT NOTICE...I WAS THINKING THAT YOU MEANT FUN AND GAMES...NOW, I REALLY HAVE TO COME UP WITH SOMETHING...ESPECIALLY, WHEN YOU SAY IT MUST BE FUNNY!" "GIRL," SHE COO'D, "YOU CAN DO ANYTHING THAT YOU MAKE UP YOUR MIND TO DO!" **BUILD UP~~BIG TIME**!!...AND WHILE SHE HAD ME WAY OUT THERE...I SAID, "WHAT DO YOU WANT ME DO, MISS. CLEMMIE?"

"I DON'T KNOW," SHE SAID...**JUST KEEP IT LIGHT... SOMETHING FUNNY...CAUSE I WANT IT TO BE FUN**!!

I STARTED THINKING~~SOMETHING FUNNY~~SOMETHING FUNNY...**ALL IN MY SLEEP**... SOMETHING FUNNY~~SOMETHING FUNN-NY!! THESE **"FUNNY"** CONVERSATIONS MADE ME THINK ABOUT A MAN WHO COMES ON RADIO...AND I HAVEN'T BEEN ABLE TO FIGURE OUT WHAT HIS ISSUES ARE...BUT HE JUST SAYS "**FUNNY! WHO'S FUNNY? AM I FUNNY?**...

FUNNY! FUNNY! WHO'S FUNNY? WHAT'S FUNNY?
FUNNY! FUNNY! AM I FUNNY!" I COULD VISUALIZE
HIM WITH FACIAL DISTORTIONS...BECAUSE I HAD A
FEW CONTORITIONS OF MY OWN...**NOW**...I THINK I AM
GETTING HIS MEANINGS!
WELL...I CAN'T BE FUNNY...BUT I SURELY ENJOY PEOPLE
THAT HAVE A SENSE OF HUMOR. NEVERTHIELESS,
MISS. CLEMMIE BETTER FIND ME FUNNY...AND I
WON'T BLAME YOU~~IF YOU DON'T...BUT EITHER
YOU **PRETEND OR BACK** OUT OF MY WAY...CAUSE I'M
GONNA LEAVE HERE RUNNING...IF SHE DOESN'T...FIND
ME FUNNY...SHE HAS GIVEN ME MORE THAN ENOUGH
WARNING THAT THIS IS TO BE A FUN GATHERING FOR
ALL...**AND IT MUST BE LIGHT AND FUNNY!!**

YOU KNOW HOW MUCH WE HATE TO TRIP OVER
EVERYTHING TO GET TO THE PHONE...ALL OUT
OF BREATH? HELLO!~~HELLO!...AND THERE IS
THIS PAUSE? WHICH WAS ALWAYS A PUZZLE TO
ME THAT I WOULD HAVE TO SAY "HELLO" SEVERAL
TIMES BEFORE SOMEONE WOULD START TALKING...
WELL~~I FOUND OUT THE REASON WHY!! FOUR OR
FIVE PEOPLE ARE CALLED AT THE SAME TIME~~BY
TELEMARKETERS...AND WHILE ALL FOUR OR FIVE
TELEPHONES ARE RINGING...THEY ARE SITTING
THERE WAITING AND PRAYING...LIKE HUNTERS
OR FISHERMEN...FOR THE FIRST ONE TO LIFT THE
RECEIVER~~SO THEY CAN ATTACK LIKE~~PANTHERS
OR PIRANHAS...WORKING AS HIGH LEVEL~
DECEIVERS.
IT DOESN'T MATTER WHO PICKS UP...MAN OR
WOMAN~OR CHILD...YOUNG~OLD~OR SENILE...

AND COLOR IS DEFINITELY NOT RESTRICTED!! AND
WHEN TWO OR MORE PICK UP...I SUPPOSE THEY ARE
SAYING...
ENNY~MENNY~~MINNY~~MOE...THREE IS A SUCKER ON
ONE OF THESE~~FOUR. HOWEVER, INSTEAD~~WHAT
WE HEAR~IS A POLITE VOICE...COURTEOUS~AND
SWEET...SAYING..."MR. OR MISS. IGNORANT PUBLIC?...
WE WANT TO GIVE YOU SOMETHING~~FREE...
AND ALL YOU HAVE TO DO IS LISTEN TO US TRYING TO
SELL YOU ANYTHING!!~~OH WHAT A COMMISSION IT
WILL BRING!"
WELL...MISS. CLEMMIE HAD ME SO CHARGED
ON THIS..."FUNNY THANG'...THAT WHEN THE
TELEPHONE~RANG I'D DO MY USUAL 50 YARD
DASH...STUMBLING INTO FURNITURE~~TOES AND
FEET~GETTING SMASHED...GRABBING THE PHONE...
LIFTING THE RECEIVER...INSTEAD OF MY NORMAL
"HELLO"...I GASP~~FUNNY~! FUNNY~ WHAT'S FUNNY!
AM I FUNNY! WHO'S FUNNY? FUN-NY!

MRS. CLEMMIE CALLED ME AGAIN...I THINK SHE WAS
CHECKING UP ON ME TO SEE WHAT I CAME UP WITH...
THAT WAS FUN AND FUNNY...SO SHE WITH CARE AND
COY~~SAID, I AM WORKING ON MY PROGRAM...WHAT
ARE THE NAMES OF THE POEMS~~THAT YOU HAVE
FOR US TO~~ENJOY? I KNOW SHE NOTICED THE LONG
SILENCE...BUT WHAT SHE DIDN'T KNOW...I WAS BITING
MY TONGUE~~TO KEEP FROM HAVING AN OUTBURST
OF~~~FUNNY? **WHAT'S FUNNY...AM I FUNNY? FUNNY!
FUNNY! WHO'S FUNNY?** FINALLY SHE SAID, "YOU
KNOW...I WANT IT TO BE FUN...WE DON'T WANT...
NOTHING HEAVY~~OR WE DON'T WANNA HAVE TOO
THINK~!...AND WHEN SHE HUNG UP~~I THOUGHT~~**ME**

NEITHER...!!! CAUSE MY MIND HAS GONE ON~A 'FUNNY FUN' BLINK!!

BUT FUNNY? WHAT'S FUNNY...AM I FUNNY? CAN I BE FUNNY? WHAT'S FUNNY? AND A LITTLE VOICE SAID, TRYING TO HELP ME WITH MY...DOUBT...REMEMBER WHEN YOU PUT YOUR TEENAGE GRANDSON`OUT?... HE WAS GOING THRU THE PUBERTY AGE...THE SWAGGERING POSTERIOR...LOOSE TONGUE...AND **TALKING BACK-SMACK-PHASE.** AND AFTER YOU HAD ONE OF THOSE~~TERRIBLE DAYS~~AT WORK...WHEN EVERYBODY GETS A PIECE OF YOUR GOOD NERVE? BUT~THIS LITTLE PIECE~~YOU HAD HELD IN RESERVE...FOR YOURSELF...BUT~~I'LL BE A 'DAMSEL FROM ITALY'...IF HE DIDN'T SNATCHED THAT LAST LITTLE BIT...AND WHEN HE DID...IN THAT MOMENT...YOU NEEDED A DOSE OF RITALIN...OR MOONSHINE~~FULL OF WINE...AND A STICK~~FOR HIS BEHIND!!
YOU TRIED TO DO A LOUD SCREAM...BUT IT CAME OUT AS A HOARSE HISSING "GET YOUR THINGS AND...GET OUT NOW...FOLLOWING BEHIND HIM...I THOUGHT FOR A MINUTE~~YOUR BODY AND THE SOUL WOULD BE DISMISSING...AND WHEN HE SAW YOUR BULGING EYES...AND FLAILING ARMS!...HE FELT THAT ONE OF YOU WAS...GONNA DIE!...WELL...HE GOT BUSY~~RUNNING REAL FAST...A BLUR OF LEGS~~WAS THE LAST TO PAST...**GIT! HISS HISS...GIT!! HISS HISS... YOU THINK YOU'RE GROWN...SO BE GONE!"** AND THEN AFTER HE HAD DISAPPEARED...A **BIG LONG-G HISSING...GIT-T-T!**

YES, HE GOT HIS BAG IN HAND~~AND RAN...OUT OF
THE GATES...BUT YOU JUST KNEW THAT HE WOULD
GO...STRAIGHT TO ONE OF HIS SISTERS...AND STAY.
BUT AFTER A FEW DAYS...THE EVENING WAS LATE...
THE HOLY SPIRIT GAVE YOU A GLIMPSE...OF
SOMETHING GOING ON~~IN THE ..'OK' CORRALS...
SOMETHING LIKE A SKIRT TAIL~~OF A GAL??...AND
AFTER PURSUING YOUR INCLINATION TO CHECK
OUT~~AND UNDER CLOSE SCRUTINY~~YOU HAD NO
DOUBT...WHAT THIS WAS ALL ABOUT!!

WELL, YOU WERE SHOCKED...AT WHAT YOU SAW IN
THIS ROOM...A PARTICULAR SPOT...WHERE THE **BOY**
HAD PAINTED THE WALLS LIKE A MURAL...A STREAK
OF DIFFERENT COLORS OF PAINTS-DONE IN FREE
FORM~~A BACKDROP FOR AN OLD COT...AN OLD
COLORED RUG ON THE DIRT FLOOR...AS YOUR EYES
TRAVEL FROM THE~~DOOR...OF THIS MAKE BELIEF
DORM...YOU WERE FILLED WITH~ EMOTIONAL
FUROR...AND DISBELIEF!! A BROTHEL, THERE IN
THE STABLES...RIGHT UNDER YOUR NOSE~AND VERY
CLOSE...A "WHOOPEE SPOT IN OLE 'OKAY CORRAL...
COULDN'T TELL HOW LONG HE HAD ENTERTAINED
THE GALS!
IT LOOKED LIKE QUITE SOMETIME FOR HIS...SECRET
RETREATS, BUT THEN THIS TIME YOU DIDN'T PLAY...
YOU BOUGHT A **GREYHOUND** TICKET...**ONE WAY**...PUT
HIM ON IT AND SENT HIM TO HIS MAMA...ENDING
THIS MESSA-RAMA!

FUNNY...WHO'S FUNNY? FUNNY! FUNNY! AM I FUNNY...
WHAT'S FUNNY?

WELL, HOW ABOUT THIS ONE~WHEN JOHN-MARK WAS
A TODDLER...AND YOU WERE TRYING POTTY-TRAIN
HIM...YOU DIDN'T MIND HIM KEEPING HIS BOTTLE...
REMEMBER...I SAID TO YOU, "WELL THAT'S ALRIGHT...
DON'T GET SO UPSET...HE WEARS THEM, **WHATCHA
CALL'EM**? **PAMPERS**!!...AND YOU GOT SO IRATE AND
SHOUTED, "PAMPERS? PAMPERS?...YES...AND I'M TIRED
OF HOISTING...THIS BOY UP...LIKE A DUMP TRUCK!
WHEN IN HIS PAMPERS...HE ERUPTS...AND SOMETIMES
THEY'RE...JUST NOT AMPLE...AND I HAVE TO USE
SPECIAL CARE...WHEN HE IS WEARING~A PAIR...NO
FAST MOVES DO...I DARE!"

SO, FINALLY...YOU MADE UP YOUR MIND~~HE WOULD
BE TRAINED THAT VERY SAME DAY!
YOU PUT HIM ON THE POTTY DISCUSSING IT WITH
HIM IN BABY GIBBERISH...MAKING IT SOUND LIKE...
ANOTHER FUN WAY TO PLAY...

BUT EVERY FEW MINUTES...HE WAS BUSY GETTING
OFF TO GET HIS TOY...BECAUSE HE THREW IT FOR THIS
VERY REASON...BEING A VERY ACTIVE...LITTLE BOY!
OR HE'D BOUNCE UP TO PICK SOMETHING...FROM OFF
THE FLOOR AND YOU KEPT JUMPING UP~TO PUT HIM
BACK ON GROUND 'P'...DO YOU REMEMBER WHEN YOU
GOT TIRED OF THIS AGGRAVATING CHORE?...AT LAST
PLUMPING HIS LITTLE 'HINNY' DOWN ON THE CHAIR...
TIED HIM DOWN WITH A TOWEL...SAYING "NOW
THERE!" DELIBERATELY, IGNORING HIS HOWLS? AND
WITH A SIGH...YOU SAT AND CLOSED~~YOUR EYES!
AND YOU HAD NO PLANS OF LETTING HIM UP THIS
TIME...BECAUSE IN THE PAST HE'D JUMPED OFF OF
THE BRIM...REAL FAST...AND A PEW~EE TRAIL OF DARK

SPOTS...WOULD FOLLOW HIM~~WHICH SHOULD HAVE
BEEN LEFT IN THE POT...!!

REMEMBER...WHEN THE BOY GOT STUCK
UNDERNEATH THE TABLE OF THE...TV...BECAUSE HE
HOPPED AROUND WITH THE ATTACHED POT...AND
YOUR PASTOR'S WIFE CALLED~~AND HEARD HIM
SHRIEK...AND YOU WERE TRYING TO UNTANGLE HIM
FROM BENEATH THE STAND~~ELECTRIC CORD AND
THE WALL?
AND YOU HEARD A BIG BOOMING VOICE SAYING,
"WHAT'S WRONG WITH JOHN-MARK?" AND YOU
SAID WITH TIMIDITY..."HE'S STUCK UNDER THE TV
STAND"..."STUCK!? STUCK!?...HOW!?...SHE BARKED...
AND YOU SAID, MEEKLY, "I TIED HIM TO HIS POTTY."
AND SHE JUMPED THRU...THE PHONE AT YOU..."CUT
HIM A LOOSE, NOW!...YOU OUGHT TO BE ASHAMED
OF YOURSELF!" REMEMBER THAT? ~~ HA! SHE COULD
TALK BIG...CAUSE SHE DIDN'T HAVE THE PROBLEM.
EVEN YOU HAD THOUGHT THAT THESE EN-COUNTERS
WERE OVER FOR YOU, TOO! NEVERTHELESS~YOU
MUSTERED UP A GOOD COME BACK~~WITH A
SIGH~~AND SAID, ~~RESPECTFULLY~~AND NO ONE
COULD DENY, "I GUESS I'LL HAVE TO BRING HIM OVER
FOR YOU~~TO POTTY TRAIN!" WITH A BIG HUFF OF
WIND, SHE SAID..."**BRING HIM ON THEN**!"
YEAH, RIGHT!!~...SHE WAS ALREADY ON OXYGEN...
COULDN'T YOU SEE JOHN-MARK WORKING THAT LAST
BIT OF AIR...WITH NO MINUTES TO...SPARE?

WELL YOU CAVED IN THAT NIGHT...DEFEATED~~**NIGHT
NOTHING**...THE SUN HAD NOT, YET, GONE DOWN. I
HEARD YOU MURMURING...WHEN YOU THREW HIM IN

HIS BUNK...THE BIRDS OUTSIDE OF YOUR WINDOW...
WAS SINGING AND HUMMING...AS YOU FLUNG YOUR
FULLY CLOTHED BODY ON YOUR BED...FEELING
AND LOOKING LIKE A PIECE OF~~HEAVY LEAD...
BREATHING HARD AND SLOWLY~~I HEARD YOU SAY,
"I REFUSE TO GO THRU ANOTHER DAY...LIKE THIS
ONE~~AND MORE~~I'LL JUST HAVE TO CLEAN YOUR
BEHIND 'TILL YOU'RE GROWN...OR "TIL I DIE..." AND, OF
COURSE~~**YOU LIED**!!!
**FUNNY!~~FUNNY? WHO'S FUNNY? WHAT'S FUNNY? AM I
FUNNY?**
FUNN~~Y!
WHAT'S FUNNY? FUN-NY!

DISTRACTIONS

Ambling along on a journey of peace~
And harmonious~living...
When suddenly~~a gentle breeze is felt...
and a soft tender whisper~is heard...and Oh-oo~
such sweetness emerge~~
with beautiful expressions...and utterance of~love!

It penetrates the façade of complacency...
With swirling emotions~reactions...
But experience and wisdom define it as a fallacy...a myth...
a mirage~of intense distractions.

Diversion in all forms are always present...
since the beginning of~~time
when earth~~knew no crime...Until...
The wicked detractor deceived Adam and Eve
and became their fatal attraction.

God had made them a beautiful home~~for them to roam~~
a joy of life without monotony~~or strife...
An environ of love~~to enjoy and explore with all of their~~heart.
Animals, mountains, hills and valleys...
Were, also, an integral~~part.
There was no worry about~~attire...just follow his laws~
and comply.

No need to have concern for designer's~clothes
[o']-naturel skins...were the original dress~~code...as they
Preened and pranced~~where everything~~showed
This was trendy until the knowledge of sin~~came in.
He made fruits...herbs~~and even fancy treats~~
for them to eat...
Yea! Well satisfied~~in this awesome~~paradise~~~
But...suddenly! A writhing head appears...
eyes focusing on the woman...
And with a cunning smile~~he verbalized...
talking his smack...creating a psychological~~impact...
As she included the man~~in this irrational~~pact.

Because of this interaction~~their paradise was lost...
And curses inundating thru generations~paid the cost...
For these sinful and wicked~~distractions.

And the heavenly living~~was cast in oblivion...
When she stopped to the level~~of the devil.
Being bewitched by the white of his eyes...
and big black lies...
Believed her life could be~~ much better!!
Paraphrasing, 'If you listen to me...
and follow my words to the~letter
We can own this world~~together!!'
Further implying~that God was lying~~
if she disobeyed...There would be no dying.
This rebellious infraction created centuries~~of distraction...
But...Jesus coming to earth~~was Father God's~reaction...

Sometimes~when life is at an acceptable~~peak
And there's no excitement~~on this journey to~~seek...

Then...suddenly!...a shooting star will leap into the heart...
Bearing down~~ relentlessly~~
Breaking the silence of~~contentment...
Igniting...passions~~and propelling emotions~~into actions.
While, uncertainty looms like a black cloud~on this path...
A strange awareness~arises...to summon the senses~~
Promising surprises~~full of mysteries...
Is it to be taken seriously?
There was no purported request in~~prayer...
Since, a fascinating career is~~being prepared.

But now...the issues of temptations...with sweltering passionate
~~awakenings...raise questions~~
whether personal integrity can sustain~~or
will it be~~forsaken.

Exciting episodes were in remission...until the stirring of
reminiscence...of Yesteryear's torrid rapture~~desired to be
recaptured...
So what's up with this~~yearning to be immersed in~~
Ecstatic~bliss??
Even with acquired wisdom and knowledge...
The memory revives endearing~frolics.

Howbeit...the legendary query of Sarah~~still resounds thru
generations..."At this age, will I again~~have pleasure?"
God answered with~reproof...
But still confirmed His words of~~truth...
And gave her the promised gift~previously, decided~
Which comes in the covenant seed~~of Isaac.

The rational is~~irrational!
Too many irreconcilable differences!!!
The age of maturity exalts the purity of life...

And the calescent breath of youth...exudes the spirit
of~fire...But~~
Medals of Prudence...Serenity and Confidence...on
the journey of~~life...
Are earned...while traveling rugged paths of difficulties...
and bitter strife.
Evenso, chasms of differentia persists...and acts as a gate~
Between ages...levels and~~devils.

Experience and wisdom~~struggle
To resist the desire of an irrepressible~~fervor...
Proper perspectives must be channeled...
To negate the natural urges~~of uncontrollable passions
Which are merely distractions~~amatory distractions
Nevertheless, when emotional thoughts are swirling...
With wild wind of~fantasies...
Undaunted judgment and sheer determination~
will conquer this fever~of ecstasy.
It is foolishness...masking in a web of~~delusions...
And illusion indulging in giddy~conclusions.
It is simple~~reactions to...impermissible distraction!

Age on either side of the spectrum~~has the melody of
The same~~song...
Whether it's from the area of wisdom...or the jubilant ballad~~
of the young...
The strains and range of~~desire...
Is like a burning torch of~~fire...acting as a stimuli...
Fusing the two...that totally disregard the time frame~~
between generations...
The thought is...UNADULTERATED HALLUCINATIONS!!!

What if...suddenly, the souls are unleashed
and become free~in the restricted time zone...
and all things become possible~~
Issues are resolvable and ideals are~~conceivable.
The bondage of inhibitions...are gone!
There is a flowing of peace~~nothing exists...
Except hearts made younger in the midst...
of vibrating waves~~and timelessness...
Palpitating as one...dancing in the~sun...
Being enraptured in bellows of emotions...
Like a churning~~ocean...
Whirling into the floodgates of love~~captured there...
in the essence of the moment...with perfect satisfaction.
HOW CAN THIS BE!!
Oh my! What fabrication of one's imagination...
These are just distractions~~*thrilling* distractions!!!

Suppress urges are beginning to surge...
A loving arm...sweet words...maybe a kiss!
Aah-h! There are no reasons strong enough to resist an electrifying
force~~demanding to be recognized...
And refuses to be hidden...and kept under~disguise!!
A decision must be made~~it cries! Choose!!
There is no need for permission...
Will it be a daily humdrum of complacency...
Or the thrill of~~energetic passions...
Oh what distraction!~~distractions...poetic distractions!

This phase of being in a daze...must soon past. How long can the
intensity
of these struggles~~last?

The ambivalence must stop! Control of these firey energies must be kept
in abeyance...and a lid put on the~~steaming pot!!

Caution cannot be thrown to the wind~~
nor years of pent up emotions be~~rescind
Pleasurable reactions to desires~only...**is crass!!**
Step aside~~let it pass!
It's only a distraction~~an enkindled distraction!

Bringing to mind~~something similar in kind...
Happened in biblical~~times;
While in an impressionable moment...David fought with his~~flesh...
As he watched Bathsheba~~undress.
Her body had a gleaming~glow...in the shimmering pool~~
just below...So he moved closer...!
Ah-h!! Her beauty was more than he could~~take...
Panting as he peeped...this act was destined~~
to put his kingdom~~at stake.

As the emotions and flesh started~~to war .,.
David stood...immobilized~~with awe...
And, then, concluded...right or wrong...He couldn't resist...
The desire was, too, strong.
Bathsheba's body and grace~~overwhelmed him with vivid
imaginations!!...as his heart raced~with strong palpitations!!

When Satan opened the door...to consummate David's~desire...
He caused him...to further~conspire...
To use his authority and skill~~and have her husband~killed...
While fighting on the battlefield.
Of course...his motive was...to conceal the evil deed...

that Bathsheba was pregnant~~with his unwanted~seed...
So he attempted to cover the atrocity~~with crafty
deceit...

So, God took the child out of his life...and caused it~to expire
Consequently, these irrational acts~~filled David's days with...
Miserable distractions...awful~~distractions...
heartrending ~~distractions!!

As King...he caused innocent blood to be~~shed
Soon...blood and shame was required...on his children's
head~and bed.
Rebelliousness~~rape and murder~replaced family love~instead...
Following a generational curse~~of suspicion and distrust.
God's exaction...for David's terrible deeds of~~infractions
which were all vain actions~~without satisfaction...
Distractions...indeed~~wicked distractions!

If purpose and destiny are in focus...the turbulence of emotional
storms
will pass~~over...
But, Oh-h...how the ocean beat of urges roar...
When the calescent winds~blows~~stirring up the soul...
making it~soar.
However...this will soon subside~into wistful patches...
Because they're only distractions~~*frantic* distractions!!

Just imagine...being alone...and without a~phone...
Slow~ly...awakening~to the whisper...of a tender love~song...
Or the sweet embracing with tender words of poetry~in a vibrant
but, soft monotone.

Can it be possible? Can it be true? That a door to the heart~~was left
slightly~~ajar...For the entering of...a gentle and tender aura~~
of refreshing innocence?

How can this be? Miles in distance of time an experience~~divide.
Evenso...the strong sentiments and desire~~resist the powerful
instinct to manifest these fervent...and passionate drives!!
However, a romantic persona~can dream of schemes...
To make these impelling forces a possibility~~it seems...
As they scream for release...to emerge and be complete!!
Oh-h! what is this?
Distraction...distractions~romantic distractions.

Howbeit...stupidity at any age is foolishness and full of~woe...
But there is something weird...lurking behind~~the evolving
door...When sensation and sensitivity~appear...
at a time when tradition says~~'It ain't~so!'

It can be concluded...that each one sets the age~zone...
frigid...torrid .. temperate...parking...stop and~go on.
Specific numbers of age...does not control the emotional~range...
It is the will of the heart that desire~change...
to perform in that...which appears~~strange.

Sometimes, the hand of fate deals vicious
and unexpected~blows...
As when Jacob labored for seven years~~
doing arduous~chores...
in exchange for the hand of Rachel~~who he had~~proposed.
But was manipulated and beguiled...when her father~lied...and
switched sister Leah, with 'tender~eyes'...to be first in the marriage

bed~~instead!
Of course, this little diversion used~~was to add seven more years~~
of servitude.
Needless to say, Jacob's heart was broken~~by this play...
Which interrupted his anticipated~~joy.

However..."What's love got to do with it?"...when circumstances are
Unpredicted...satisfactions are nil...unjust actions~~are surreal...
Hey!! It's only another distraction...merely distractions!

Subsequently, Rachel swapped Jacob for her nephew's~~
mandrake...
Tent sharing~then...is the same today...
play on common ground...and participate...
The familiar cry on an action block is~~
Gather all the flock...Catch while you can...
Trade up or down~for the phallus of the~~Man!

Howbeit...life is not a perfect package...and some offenses
Cannot be eradicated~~from the haven of good...
Nor is there a bottled remedy to satisfy~~until we die...
which is understood!
And when troubles and struggles are interspersed~~
happiness...peace and joys~~quickly disperse.
Nevertheless...who lights up our path on the way...
As we travel on our journey of no returning?
The time spent day-by-day~is not always smooth...and
many hurdles are on the path of golden~~rules!
But be encourage~~as Jesus continue to~~urge...
He is in every moment of awakening~
When the roots of hope~are shaken...

Nevertheless...the Holy Ghost is here...
When trouble starts~~and life becomes, too, hard...
'He is the lamp on our feet and the light~~on our path'...
When the way is turning~dark.
And our lives are built on~that hope...in~~Father God~
and the Lord Jesus!

Howbeit...distractions~~are all a part of~life...
intertwined and intermingled~~with emotional
Turmoil and~strife...
Nevertheless...help is under the umbrella~~of the Holy Spirit...
As He protects us and never grows~~weary.
Yet...Distractions will be constant trespassers...
Some are happy...others are sad...
And more than a few~~makes us~~mad!!
However...there are those that can be~~reconciled...
And put in neat little piles...
Of romantic bliss and sweet~~dreams~~
Which sometimes boost~~our self-esteem!
Ah-h-h...but none is like enraptured ecstasy~~
of a passionate distraction.

Whatever~the circumstances~~nothing enhances...
Like the anticipation~of an exciting~~romance...
Nor the encounter with supernatural forces~of love...
Emanating from~above...
Howbeit...Distractions are necessary experiences~~
to gain wisdom...knowledge~~and understanding...
Which leads to peaceful and spiritual expansion...
After the passage of~~these Distractions!!...

Nevertheless, in every phase of life~~
We have trials and tribulations...
And distractions~~of many distractions!

AGERS

Seemingly...we are caught up in this "Age Thang"...
And when the 'younguns' come into the world...
Everything begins to~change.
They are rushing thru...being grown~before their time...
Fastly...turning the pages~~of ages...
As we dwindle~~while in our prime.

However~each age group has its own distinction...
and in all levels...there are stepping stones~~
Which lead to paths of~~right and wrong.

Nevertheless...to reach the appointed destiny~~
It is essential...
To break the hold of the...Tempter...
Who is trying to control~~in dark suspension.
So, our Holy hands...must continue to press...
To be relieved of this~~hellish stress!

At the head~of the clever schemes~of 'AGER'...
Is the little cunning infant...
Who comes in kicking and raging...
E'nuf~~already...making parents...crazy!
Demanding to be fed~~rocked~~and 'ditey' changed...
Never mind~whether you're in pain...
On its specified time~~your world~~hang.

Whether in the position of standing tall...
or~bending~limping~~and ready to fall...
Trying to see thru eyes~~that lack sleep.
But just cater to 'Baby Ager'...and win a prize...
To another side~~that's sugary sweet!
And~be aware...this first rage...is the take over stage.

Finally...'Baby Ager' graduates to a~~'Toddler Ager'
Breaking thru in~hot defiance~~a real challenger...
That refuses to be~~in compliance.

And even tho'...this is a two to five year~~phase...
Parental control is a necessity~~to embrace...
And unify~~as JOINT CHIEFS OF STAFF...
To stand against~~the child's wrath.

Now...a "YOUNG AGER"~~around eight~
Nine thru twelve...is in a daze...
Trying to fit into...the people maze.

It is challenging to direct a child into...
The proper 'age' category~~
Which once upon a time...is my story...
Expressing the status...of his teenage~progression~
Was quite~impressive.
As he confronted me~with a little cocky stance
About the up and coming...school dance.

"What you can't trust me for one hour?"
As he squinted up at me...
"Son, the spirit is willing...but the flesh

is weak...demons have power...while your
conscience sleeps!"

"You may think...and feel it~Son...
But at the age of Eleven...
You are just fresh~~from Heaven.
The talking to girls on the phone...
Is like being in the twilight zone...on 'La La Land'
And means far more...than you can~~understand!

Your young age...is not nearly done...
And later when you reach~~your teens...
This will be a time...to have some fun...
Have dreams...indulge in a few illusions...
Strive for conclusions...and resist confusions."

Well...he said..."then I am a ~ 'YOUTHAGER'"

'Hum-m!~~Now...I'll accept that!
Because it's closer...to being a fact!"

Now...A TEENAGER~~covers the stormy 'age'...
Of Thirteen~thru Nineteen...
And sets new stages...for the hormonal~rage.

They can be obnoxious and~unkind...
Thinking parents are crazy...and lived
In "primitive"~~ time.
Even tho'...we survived their shriekings~~
from the cradle...Puberty landslides~of pivotal ages...
And other menacing ways...that were unstable.
When the children are~'ADULT AGERS'~~
Making choices and decisions...

And there are no parent/child~schism...
Then, we all have arrived~
To live separate lives...
We all are grown~~
And thanks to the Lord~~they all are gone!

The conclusion of this confusion...begins
As soon as...we are ejected from~the womb...
And on our way to the~tomb...
We challenge~~our parents...
We are lamps~~defined...
With lights that shine...
And as minuscule's...hop out of the~~cradle...
As soon as we're able~~
To point fingers of accusations.

The hormones rules the mind...
Causing body parts...to be unaligned...
Creating an atmosphere~of stringency...
Competition~~that's a contingency...
Until~finally...with resiliency...
We evolve as~~ONE WITH THEM...
Thusly...as a~~

"MIDDLE AGER"...All dignified and purified...
Throwing previous wicked attributes...
upon the shelf...not looking back...at that part...
of our self...

For we want our children to remember~
The picture...
Of a pious life and~~existence...
Being born purified...sanctified~~Holy~and...
Never lied!

And finally!~~Oh Lord!...thank you
for bringing me~thru...
On to the stage~~of 'OLD AGER'...
Uh-excuse me!...*Interpretation*...
Guiding me into the phase~~of senior maturation...

However...on this plane...there is a subtle~~
Invasion~of feelings of change...
known as the 'Senior Thang'!
Evenso...the labeling of~"Senior Citizen"...
is an irritation.

Being a mother...of all these ages...
For many years of tears...
And suddenly...not awaken to freedom~
But instead~another title...has to be worn...
Which is blighted hope...on a wider scope.

Health challenges...are more binding and confining...
And a different kind of whipping~stick...
No more shouting and screaming~~
Shortness of breath causes a whisper...
No more walking briskly...you toddle...
Stiff joints have to be...coddled!

So~~the labeling...of battle worn warriors~~
As "Senior Citizens"...isn't necessary.
Memories~~of sacrifices~~
Are medals...sustained...
And manifested~continually
in many aches~~and pain...

Now~~! When 'Discounts' are involved...
And other offers of special favors...
Which~~of course...respects contributions~~
Of past~~labors...
Then...it's time to join in the gang...
Of the 'Senior Thang'!
And confess~~"I am blessed"!!

There are days...when an extra few minutes~
are necessary...
To get from point 'A'~to point 'Z'...
And squinting is essential~~to see.

It is a nuisance to lie down~
Just to rest your back...
When luggage has to be packed...
And wood needs to be stacked...

Going slower...and Staying focus~~
Is a bother...
Nevertheless...All praises and thanks...go to
Our father.

The running~jumping~swinging of the skirts...
Has turned from tipping...to-ing and fro-ing
To dipping and groping...
And the bold walk~while swaggering...
Has turned to a~low stoop...

With pants bagging...and skirt sagging...
From a jogging walk...and a mild lope~~
To carefully planted steps~~
On a rising...slope...

'cause...By now...everything aches!...
Back~feet~corns...and~bunions...
At this age~who cares...
About a breath smelling~like onions.
And at this point...my advice is:...don't push
Helping arms away...let them lin'ger~r~r
If he is handsome...
Maybe...this could be the~~answer...
To refute the 'big bang'...of the 'Woman
Lib Thang.'

Leaping and loping~~like an agile antelope
Has changed to a careful~grope
on a hand rail~~or rope...
Bad days are good...for staying home~~
Learning skills...on how to cope...
And resist the dastardly pull~~of gravity.
Hey!~~The rest of life~~should be lived~~
Lavishly!

An important suggestion...on survival...
Before sitting in a chair...grab it firmly...
And hold it...be sure it's~there!
Then...slowly~~let your body descend~~
To the front of the seat~~right to the end...
Hold on~~for 'dear life!'...
Sliding back...for a safer contact...
To avoid a painful~~impact.
No more...just plopping down!
Keep the body~~off the ground.
However~some of the pride and cuteness...
Is still around...
But kept in control...and astuteness.

Oh! What you say? I'm still like a young foal...
Heh~~heh~~yeah~h!
Aw-w~! You say getting 'ole'~~
Whatcha mean?
Who me?~~Eh?
I'm just shivering...maybe catching~~a cold.

Yep! ,,, Sho do! kerri mi fan eber what~I goz!
Whi? Whi?...cause it's in fashin'~~dat's whare!!
Sho ain't non of dem...what'cha kall'm~~

Yeah...Yeah!~Hort flashin'
Naw-w~! Ise fanni'...kaus'~~
Ise fill wid~~Passhin!!
Drest tuh~kil'...fillin' dicti...fied...
An' kool as a pea!

O'lawdy! heah he cums...start'n at mi feet...
Muvin' on up mi legs...and thi's...
Gittin' me hott'n~fie!!...
He's cummin' on up~tuh mi fais...
Ise dun pul ofn mi coat an'~~swetters...
Mi swet~~Ise star'n tuh~tase...
Ise star'n snatchin' awf mi udder...attie...

Den! Ise cum tuh mi sins...an'hurri fur mi wepon...!
Tun it own~fas'...and' gibe hem~
ar cole shot~ob ai'!
An' den he vanis...Jes lik' he neber ben~heah!

Ole Agiur?...Is dat whut yuh kal me?
Wel'...Ise hab yuh tuh no~~Ise a "No Agier"~

Dat's goin' thu lebels of matuui-dy...
Ef~we lib lon' Ion 'nuf...dat's uh shure-ty!!

Is sta' own mi ben'n nees~wid Psalm 71:9~~
It says..."Cast me not off in my old age;
for sake me not when my strength faileth!!

And ise stan' own de pramus ob Issaih...46:4
an' it sa'~~"Even to your old age...I am he and
even to hoar hairs~will I carry you...I have
made and I will bear~even I will carry and will deliver you.

Yes~ss!...I'M 'AGELESS!!!

THE BATTLE BELONGS TO THE LORD

Who is the tall...strong...and dedicated
Young man?
Is it David that has manifested himself~~once again...
Taking the reins of deliverance...
To save the children of Israel?

Or is he the appointed lad...that's chosen to be
Leader and comrade...
Who suffered from heartache and pain...
While walking through the jungle of
Turbulent storms of rejection...with tears~~
flowing like rain...
Even Satan's laughter~playing his old familiar game...
Could not stop the destiny...of being selected~and ordained

No~we can't wash our hands as Pilate did...releasing
Responsibility of the challenge~to fight...
For what is right...
No...we can't shake the dust from our feet~in defeat...
It is Jesus' love~that encourages us to stand~
As he guides us with his hand~~to serve him...
Making our journey...a path of learning.
He hung on the cross...
Freely~shedding his blood...then rising above...
Taking away all reasons...for us to be loss.

Jesus has already taken our tasks and burdens...
So we could walk in His presence...
He shines his light...behind the curtain of evil darkness...

And beckons us with his love...while breaking Satan's chain~of
Mockery!

"Be not dismayed"...He says..."I am the way...
And in my footsteps...follow me~~all of your days!"
"And as I lead...you follow me...and as I give you utterance...
Speak it to my people!
I am the **way**...the **truth**...and the **light**.

"Behold...I will come as a thief in the night...to take my
People back...
Where Satan and his demons...can no longer attack...
The pits of HELL~is their DOOM!...
Thereby will be consumed!
Then my children will be free to roam...in their prepared room...
Where there is no more Sadness~Sickness~Stress...
Nor DEATH!"

JESUS LOVES YOU AND SO DO I
PASTOR E.W. BAGBY!!!

Evangelist Henrietta Davison, Poetess

THE CONCLUSION

My father, I thank you in the name of your Holy Son, our Lord Jesus, empowered by the Holy Spirit for enabling me to bring this Book to conclusion!

Jesus, my Lord and Savior, I thank you for being within me with your power, light, hope and strength; that allow me to do all things through you, because you live within me.

Holy Ghost, I thank you for guiding me in my writings and every facet of my life: I thank you for being my Comforter, Counselor, Interpreter, my Teacher, my Writer and being all things to me, while I lean on you ... and in You!

Holy Spirit, I pray that you anoint the Readers of this Book with spiritual perception, as you have anointed my writings.

I thank you Holy Ghost, with my whole "Being," for the teachings and spiritual insight ~ for every word and sentence...that you gave me to use in this Book...not only will it touch the spirit of others, but it enhanced and advanced my spirituality as well! I hunger and thirst after your righteousness...and your blessing of spiritual knowledge; to learn... to teach and share with others. I thank You!

Lord Jesus let your Holy Light shine through these writings and let your love, strength and healing of the mind, body and soul...touch every person that reads this Book!

Father God, I thank you for my family and friends, who took the time to write 'encouraging comments' and make 'verbal statements' of support for the addendum of this book. Father...from the reading of them; I am going to stay on bending knees in supplication to you, so I can one day, be able to fulfill these accolades of such heartfelt sentiments.

Father God...bless us, indeed...enlarge our borders...keep your hands upon us and keep us from evil and from doing evil...so that we may not be grieved and that we may not grieve you!! Thank you for hearing Jabez's prayer and mine ~ and answering it!

I thank you my dear Father and Lord Jesus for opening the door of Dr. Maya Angelou's heart and home...permitting me and my friends, Joyce Duren and Barbara Charles...to enter-visit- and exchange Books... as if we were equally on her social level! Her maid served coffee and tea as we chatted like old friends. I had wanted to meet her, since being compared with her delivery style of speaking; but I never dreamed that it would be on a personal level! And in her home? I will never forget her. She treated us like we were on her socio-status! She will always have a special place in my heart!

I give you all the glory and honor and praise...not only answering my prayer for that precious moment and time, with Dr. Maya Angelou; but also for the writing of this book...my Father God ~ Lord Jesus ~ and Holy Ghost!! I give you a shout out of praise!! Amen! Amen! Amen!

Henrietta Davison
August 10, 2015 ~ revised

Now, Father, I have brought closure to this, my first book. I give you all the praise, glory, and honor.

If anyone receives any wisdom...
If anyone receives any insight...
If anyone receives any knowledge...
If anyone can share the love of Jesus...
If anyone is enlightened...
If anyone can embrace his/her fellow men/sisters...

Then this book is not written in vain!!!

Ms. Henrietta Davison, a daughter...a mom...a grandma...an auntie...a prayer partner...and truly a friend sent by God to this "almost heavenly" place called West Virginia, to be a blessing to us all...You'll be captivated and swept into her writings as she shares her unique way in presenting life's many journeys in poetry..."Lady Davison"–As we venture into the "new millennium," God's continued blessings as you abide in His lead, and your book goes from coast to coast–blessing all as it has blest me!

Your Friend

Joyce
Duren-Seabrook

This project is the most significant investment you can make in your own potential for greatness.
Good luck.

Your Pastor and friend,

Roosevelt and Earline Neal
Kathryn and Ebony McCormick

Words of Encouragement from the Family:

Waine: Mom, I send out into the universe all the positive bless-ings one individual can possible receive. I commend you on your effort to have the will to challenge your next excursion. "May God walk with you all the way."

Andrew: Congratulations on your second book. Can't wait to own a copy of it.

Janisha: I want to congratulate you on your second book and hope it's successful.

Tashia: Congrat's on book #2 and may God bless you and be with you always.

Rhonda: I cannot wait to see you this summer. I hope to have your little blessing hooked up for you by then.

I am very happy for you. I am looking forward to the book. I even kept the little note you wrote–I'll have it when you are on T.V.–(smile).

Love You,
Leola Johnson

Verbal Statements of Support and Encouragement

Barbara LousteauCindy Irwin Bostic
Ide Belle RhyneAnita Thomas
Jacqui TaylorEthel Bivens
Alma Logan RosantaCarolyn Jones
Clarence OwensKathy Lousteau

Henrietta Davison...

This brilliant woman has touched our hearts and soul with the readings from her book of Epic poetry. Henrietta Davison is a woman on a mission to bring knowledge and wisdom to the hearts and ears of our nation. Ms. Davison's poetry provides culture and information for the people of this millennium era. I truly applaud her wonderful work of art.

Barbara L. Charles
Community Voice Newspaper
Of the Raleigh County NAACP

Henrietta Davison...what a legacy–You're indeed a role-model and encourage to our young woman who need to see and read about more accomplishments from great writers such as yourself with Christian goals and culture. Women of God, who take their lead from our Lord and Savior Jesus Christ.

Your Sister in Christ and prayer partner,
Joyce Seabrook
Author

Our dear friend, Henrietta,

We truly feel blessed simply to call you "friend." Congratulations on the writing of your second book. We know, all eyes that feast upon the children of your heart will leave your bountiful works, filled with blessings. You once told us that your writings were not you own but inspired by the Holy Spirit. The fruit of your works is proof of your statement. Your narration's bless, provoke, inspire, encourage, and some cause a smile or two often times erupting into a full belly laugh. We know as long as your heart and head are open to His Majesty your poetic gifts will endure. May God ever bless and keep you, and may our friendship be long.

Lovingly,
William and Clemmie Hinton

ENDORSEMENTS

Hi Mom,

I just want to say congratulations on your second edition, and that I'm very proud of you. I will always love ya ma, YOU ARE MY ROCK!!

I know this book will go even further than the last.

Don't work too hard tonight!

Love ya,
JC

Grace and Resoration Christian Center
P.O. Box 711
Beckley, WV 25901

Praise The Lord:

Dear Mrs. Davison, thank you for your contribution to the world in the expression of poetry. Your work has transcended time, and will be with us in many years to come. The ministry that is in you is awesome and we appreciate you. I thank God for putting you in our lives and we love you much. Keep writing under the Divine Inspiration of the Holy Spirit and many souls will be saved as you minister life in the word in the unique expression called POETRY. A TRUE 21st CENTURY BATTLE AX.

Pastors Roosevelt and Earline Neal
Ebony, Kathryn and NataiJah

Hi Henri,

What God has joined together, let no man put asunder??? Ordinarily, I would surmise this to mean the overflowing love of a man and woman betrothed in endless love and matrimony. However, to my sister in Christ, my mentor at an early age, my big sister, my mother; and at long last, to my friend; I applaud your success as a poetess.

Love and Prayers–Your Sister in Christ
Claudia Morgan

ABOUT THE AUTHOR...
By
PHYLLIS B. BEASLEY

S he came to the fork in the road. One path had many footprints, as though it had been traveled by a multitude, the other had barely a footprint in it, as if it had been less traveled.

So...she stopped to ponder which path she should take, should it be the path of a multitude of footprints? Or, should it be the one with the least footprints? She surmised that the treasures of gems and jewels had most likely been trampled, or picked over, by the traveling multitude. Her curious nature decided on the less traveled path to seek the possibility of treasures in abundance.

Along the way, she found a stone, distinct in shape and weight. She picked it up and examined it and discovered a gem; a gift of writing prose and poetry that was motivated by her belief in God and humanity.

I met Mrs. Henrietta Davison more than a decade ago, and since our first introduction, I have been inspired, blessed and comforted by her many words of wisdom. I believe that others will also be inspired, blessed and comforted, as they read her book.

She writes in a contemporary period, endowed with spirituality and possessing the tolls of empowerment of her ancestors.

Her book of prose and poetry is spiritually motivated and affirms the many blessings God plans for humanity. May God continue to guide her hands and heart as she shares these writings of inspiration and encouragement! My personal prayer for Henrietta Davison is that God bless her with peace, joy and prosperity as she works in His will.

Your trusted friend,
Phyllis

www.ingramcontent.com/pod-product-compliance
Lightning Source LLC
Chambersburg PA
CBHW031241090426
42742CB00007B/271